CANARY ISLANDS

G000295212

By the staff of Editions Berlitz

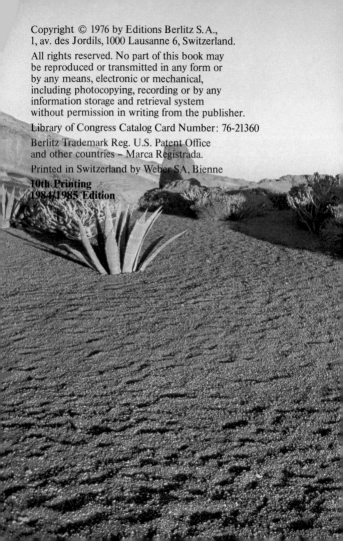

Library of Congress Catalog Card Number: 76-21360

Berlitz Trademark Reg. U.S. Patent Office
and other countries – Marca Registrada.

Printed in Switzerland by Weber SA, Bienne

**10th Printing
1984/1985 Edition**

How to use our guide

- All the practical information, hints and tips that you will need before and during the trip start on page 99, with a complete rundown of contents on page 103.

- For general background, see the sections The Islands and the People, p. 6, and A Brief History, p. 10.

- All the sights to see are listed between pages 18 and 73. Our own choice of sights most highly recommended is pinpointed by the Berlitz traveller symbol.

- Entertainment, nightlife and all other leisure activities are described between pages 74 and 91, while information on restaurants and cuisine is to be found on pages 92 to 98.

- Finally, there is an index at the back of the book, pp. 126–128.

Although we make every effort to ensure the accuracy of all the information in this book, changes occur incessantly. We cannot therefore take responsibility for facts, prices, addresses and circumstances in general that are constantly subject to alteration. Our guides are updated on a regular basis as we reprint, and we are always grateful to readers who let us know of any errors, changes or serious omissions they come across.

Text: Ken Bernstein
Photography: Daniel Vittet
Layout: Serge Tcherdyne
We are particularly grateful to Ben Gilroy for his help with this book. We also wish to thank the Spanish National Tourist Office for its valuable assistance.
Cartography: Falk-Verlag, Hamburg.

Contents

Maps

Bird's-Eye View of Canary Islands pp. 6–7, Tenerife p. 21, Santa Cruz de Tenerife p. 22, Puerto de la Cruz p. 25, Gran Canaria p. 38, Las Palmas de Gran Canaria pp. 40–41, Lanzarote p. 51, Fuerteventura p. 58, Gomera p. 63, La Palma p. 66, El Hierro p. 71.

The Islands and the People

The Canaries—seven specks scattered over 300 miles in the middle of the vast Atlantic, plus a handful of minor flecks. Yet these lonely volcanic islands encompass such a variety of features that they can evoke within a few hours' drive the beaches of Bali or the terraced mountains of Nepal, the hellfire of Hades or the pasturelands of Ireland.

To realize just where you are, you must sniff the tang of the ocean mingling with the perfume of tropical flowers. Hear the soft lilt of local music and speech. Taste fish fresh from the sea or a banana straight from the plantation. Feel the delight of warm, powdery sand between your toes—or the laughable discomfort astride a shambling camel. Stroll along vineyard paths or descend into a crater.

The Fortunate Islands, as they have been called since Antiquity, owe their fame and fortune to their geographical situation— and to the climate. Just off the African coast and aided by favourable trade winds, the Canaries grow fruit and vegetables year-round for the tables of Europe. They

PORTUGAL

OCEANO

ISLAS

N

La Palma

Gomera

El Hierro

Tenerife

also lure millions of tourists escaping the extremes of weather in less blessed latitudes. There's plenty of room for more: seven major and six minor islands* add up to an area bigger than the Hebrides or somewhat smaller than Puerto Rico.

It took the Spaniards the best part of the 15th century to subdue the Stone Age inhabitants of all the islands. Never treated as a colony, the archipelago was integrated into Spain. At the present time it's divided into two provinces administered from Santa Cruz de Tenerife and Las Palmas de Gran Canaria. The total population is about 1,300,000.

Although local culture is encouraged and the Guanche cavemen are romanticized, today's Canarians speak Spanish (with a sing-song, lilting accent), look Spanish and feel Spanish. For many visitors the only obvious difference between the islands and mainland Spain is the cost of luxuries. Formerly duty free, the Canaries' duties are still generally lower than on the mainland.

Other than that, generalizations don't work. Each island has its own dimensions and character.

---

* Plus San Borondón, a legendary isle which may have been invented to avoid a total of 13!

SPAIN   Gibraltar

MOROCCO

ATLANTICO

Lanzarote

CANARIAS   Fuerteventura

SAHARA

Gran Canaria

Tenerife, the biggest, is as lush as any tropical paradise—except for dramatic volcanic zones and Mount Teide, 12,198 feet high.

Gran Canaria is strong on beaches and swinging nightlife, but (like Tenerife) grows those famous bananas and tomatoes.

Lanzarote may sound like a melancholy memory of volcanic catastrophe, but it's gloriously black and beautiful and well provided with beaches.

Fuerteventura, beachiest of all the Canaries, is only a stone's throw from the Sahara—and looks it.

Gomera is so hilly the islanders used to communicate from crag to crag in a unique whistling language, now alas, almost obsolete.

La Palma may well be the fairest of them all—green and alluring—but its tempo is too leisurely for some tourist tastes.

El Hierro, smallest and least developed of the Canaries, is strictly for the simple pleasures—a getaway island that can claim to be world's end.

Whichever island you choose, don't neglect the very living local folklore; investigate, too, the handicrafts and, of course, try the cuisine. Try

to take in one or more of the neighbouring islands, as well. See the cathedrals, palaces and old houses built with exquisite workmanship. Go to a village festival, a mixture of faith and fanfare. Explore a cave or climb a mountain. Play golf or go shark-fishing. See a concert or dance all night. Listen to the parrots whistling at the girls.

The Canaries are more than just a winter's suntan.

Primitive elements of nature meet spectacularly in Canaries: air, earth, water and volcanic fire.

Island history is written in furrows of harsh land, faces of its people and (opposite) prehistoric graffiti.

A Brief History

Legends cling to the Canaries like the clouds enveloping Mount Teide. If no one can prove they're true, it's reassuring to know that no one can actually prove them false. Only a hopeless cynic would deny the possibility that these islands just might have been the prototype of paradise.

Homer tells us that the blessed were sent to the Elysian Fields to enjoy eternal happiness in a land where winter was unknown. Is he suggesting Zeus sent the saintly to the Canary Islands? Were they mankind's first package tourists?

The father of history, Herodotus, mentions the Garden of the Hesperides, a happy land where the sun sets. Was he thinking of Elysium, Eden or perhaps the Canaries?

Another famous author, Plutarch, hints of fertile islands somewhere off the coast of Africa where the breezes of springtime never stop. His source was the idealistic Roman leader Sertorius, who had heard it from the lips of an explorer.

Were all these authors confusing the Canaries with Atlantis? Plato does locate the lost continent to the west of Gibraltar, somewhere in the Atlantic Ocean. By Plato's computations the rich, happy island was destroyed by earthquakes and tidal waves nearly 12,000 years ago.

After the cataclysm only the mountain-tops of Atlantis remained above sea level and constituted seven islands, the Canaries. True or false? From Plato to Jules Verne, the possibilities have stirred the imaginations of writers, historians,

geologists and archaeologists, to say nothing of innumerable eccentrics. Thousands of books have been published propounding one or another theory. When you sight Mount Teide on a distant horizon, you will understand the profusion of legends.

The First Inhabitants

Long before the first European navigators beached in the Canaries, all seven principal islands of the archipelago were inhabited. The natives, called Guanches,* are thought to have arrived many hundreds of years earlier. The nagging, unsolved question remains: Where did they come from and how?

Ethnographers link them with North Africa's Cro-Magnon man. The Guanches were

* Only the aboriginal inhabitants of Tenerife can properly be referred to as Guanches. In their native language the word *guanche* simply meant man. In practice the natives of all the islands are often lumped with the Guanches for convenience.

Caves were home for natives of Canaries when Spaniards arrived.

tall, white-skinned, often blue-eyed and blond-haired. About 5,000 Guanche skulls have been excavated and studied in the hope of learning more about their origin. (Unless you're particularly squeamish, have a look at the meticulous collections of ancient skulls in the archaeological museums of Tenerife and Gran Canaria. See MUSEUMS, page 86.)

Conjecture about the Guanches has to be flexible because not all the facts will fit any one theory. For example, it's particularly difficult to explain how they learned, and why they practiced, the ritual of mummification. The Guanches embalmed their dead in the same way as the ancient Egyptians.

The Guanches were literally cavemen. Because of their isolation, they were still in the Stone Age when the first Europeans arrived. But little by little they were assimilated into the society of their Spanish conquerors. Yet evidence of the islanders' aboriginal heredity is still apparent in the number of blue-eyed, blond-haired Canarians you'll come across.

Other reminders of their past add exotic touches to the island scene: the actual caves they called home; their special food, *gofio,* which remains the Canaries staple; the games the Guanches taught their children, still played today; and the names of so many places in the archipelago—Tabaiba, Tafira, Tamadaba, Teneguia, Timanfaya, Teide and Tenerife itself.

New Arrivals

The first record of foreigners visiting the Canaries goes back 2,000 years. Subsequently, Arab sailors who landed on Gran Canaria reported that the inhabitants met them graciously. Indeed almost all travellers who came to the islands in peace left with favourable impressions. For instance, a Spanish sea-captain, shipwrecked on Lanzarote in the 14th century, eventually returned home with the happiest of memories. However, a few years earlier a landing party which included five Franciscan monks had met the ultimate in hostile receptions; they were captured and put to death. Towards the end of the 14th century an expedition from Seville had the shock of a lifetime when Mount Teide erupted before their eyes; the terrified sailors gave Tenerife an unfortunate nickname—"hell island". The nickname, like the sailors, didn't linger.

The European conquest of the Canaries, island by island, began in 1402. It proved to be more protracted and bloody than anyone had imagined, and the pacification process lasted almost a century.

The conquest began auspiciously, even festively, on the island closest to Europe, Lanzarote. The Norman baron, Jean de Béthencourt, in the service of Henry III, king of Castile, stepped ashore to a totally friendly welcome.

Béthencourt next conquered Fuerteventura, moving on in logical geographical progression to Gran Canaria, only to be thwarted by a devastating storm which scattered the invasion fleet. He never lived to rule Gran Canaria.

The baron did, however, collect one more piece of property for the crown—the farthest of the islands, El Hierro. He was strangely unchivalrous here, obtaining the surrender of the heroic native king under false pretences: he enticed the king to a peace meeting, ambushed him, and then deported him into slavery.

The Portuguese, who had already settled Madeira, the Azores and the Cape Verde Islands, began to covet the strategic and agricultural prize of the Canaries. Naval skirmishes ensued between the two powers. At the end of the succession war between Portugal and Castile, the wide-ranging Treaty of Alcaçovas of 1480 ended Lisbon's claims to "the Fortunate Islands".

Now, by order of Ferdinand and Isabella, known to Spaniards usually as the Catholic Kings, the second phase of the conquest of the Canaries was set in motion. By 1483 Gran Canaria had been subdued. Five years later, skipping the most difficult target, Tenerife, the Spaniards seized Gomera. **13**

Columbus slept here: residence of island governor, now a museum.

The World is Round!

This happened just in time for that incomparable turning point in world history, the 1492 expedition of Christopher Columbus. While the great navigator was overhauling his little fleet in Gran Canaria and stocking up with food and water in newly Spanish Gomera, two of the Canary Islands were still firmly resisting the benefits of civilization. The small green island of La Palma held out until May 1493. And La Palma's conqueror, Alonso Fernández de Lugo, needed thousands of soldiers and two years of furious fighting before the biggest island, Tenerife, was won.

Meanwhile, after sailing beyond El Hierro—the end of the known world—Columbus failed to fall off the edge. The trade winds wafted him to the Caribbean islands, an even more intriguing discovery than a new route to the Indies. Columbus's board of directors, Ferdinand and Isabella, quickly realized that America offered more exciting prospects than the Canaries.

But the role of the islands as a bridge between the Old World and the New was to continue down the centuries. Canarians have settled in Latin America in large numbers. Canarian bananas provided the stock for those of the Caribbean. In accent and music, the Canaries lie half-way between Spain and the New World. News of Venezuela or Cuba is almost a local item in the Canary Islands' press.

Wine and Warfare

The first major agricultural enterprise to put the Canaries on the world map was sugar, but, after getting off to a fine start, by the late 16th century business was terrible. It wasn't that Europeans had gone on diets, they just preferred the cheaper sugar from the West Indies.

Fortunately, a new farming venture rescued the Canaries' economy. Grapes grown in the volcanic soil produced a distinctive wine, malmsey *(malvasía),* which became *the* drink of aristocratic Europe. Shakespeare and Voltaire, among others, were lavish in their praise of this sweet white wine. (Variations on the original malmsey may be found in local *bodegas* and restaurants today, mostly in the more remote areas; some are delicious.)

By the end of the 18th century the Canaries were important enough to have attracted all manner of pirates as well as that most fearless sailor, Horatio Nelson. In search of a Spanish treasure ship said to be sheltering in Santa Cruz de

The centuries-old lure of sunken treasure still spurs exploration.

Tenerife harbour, the great admiral attacked the garrison there. The defenders, in perhaps their finest hour, defeated Nelson, killing 226 British sailors and wounding 123. In addition, the admiral's saluting arm was shot off. Nelson had his revenge at Trafalgar in 1805 when he defeated the combined French and Spanish fleets. The inhabitants of Santa Cruz de Tenerife clearly had no hard feelings, for one of their streets, the Calle de Horacio Nelson, is named after him.

Changing Directions

No sooner had Nelson trimmed Spain's sails than the armies of France invaded. Napoleon's brother, Joseph Bonaparte, seized the Spanish throne and sparked off the Peninsular War (Spaniards call it the War of Independence). England came to the aid of its former enemy and helped eject the French from Spanish soil. Volunteers from the Canaries, by now fully Spanish in outlook and loyalties, went to war alongside their mainland cousins. Independence was achieved, and in 1814 Ferdinand VII was restored to his throne.

In the 19th century the traditional one-crop economy of the Canaries took a right-angle turn down a weird agricultural byway. Big money was found in cochineal, a parasite attracted to cactus (see p.62). But with the rise of modern chemistry this lucrative insect trade collapsed, only to pick up again recently.

In an effort to help the islands, the Spanish government made a gesture in the mid-19th century, with far-reaching, even unexpected consequences: by royal decree they were proclaimed free ports. Cumbersome duties and paperwork were eliminated, encouraging maximum expansion of trade. The two main harbours, Santa Cruz and Las Palmas, were now all set to become ports of world importance.

In the Spanish-American War of 1898, Spain's last colonies in the New World were wrested from her. The formidable Spanish Empire had shrunk so dramatically that the Canaries were now its furthest western outpost. But the Canaries, unlike the colonies, were an integral part of Spain itself. In 1927 two provinces were created, Las Palmas being made capital of the eastern islands, Santa Cruz of the four westerly islands.

Modern Times

The plot which touched off the Civil War was hatched in the Canary Islands. The captain-general of the Canary Islands, in charge of all military as well as civil affairs in the archipelago, was a young general named Francisco Franco. In 1936 a group of officers, opposed to the policies of the Republican government in Madrid, secretly met with Franco on Tenerife. Franco later took off for North Africa, launching pad for the insurgent attack.

Franco's right-wing armies triumphed in a three-year struggle. But despite Hitler's endeavours to gain Franco's help, Spain remained neutral during the Second World War. This meant that the Canary Islands could not be used as bases during the Battle of the Atlantic. By 1955 passions over the Civil War and Franco's rule had tempered sufficiently for Spain to gain admission to the United Nations. In 1969 the Generalísimo set the scene for his departure by naming his polit-

Tourists spy on La Graciosa: no shortage of beaches for tomorrow.

ical heir: Prince Juan Carlos de Borbón (grandson of Spain's last king, Alfonso XIII), who became monarch and head of state in 1975.

For the Canaries, the 1960s and 1970s were a period of rapid growth. The harbours of Tenerife and Gran Canaria were clogged with freighters and tankers. Tenerife's tonnage doubled within a decade.

The greatest innovation of the 1980s has been the creation of the autonomous region of the Canary Islands, with its own local parliament. Now islanders can assume greater control over their political and economic destiny. Among other key posts, special prominence has been given to the development of tourism and transport. For Tenerife and Gran Canaria, and to a lesser degree the other islands, have been transformed by the flood of jet-package tourists: the virtual guarantee of sun and warmth all year round, in congenial surroundings, with a welcoming population and dramatic landscape are a combination of factors almost unique.

Despite the violent change in the tempo of their everyday lives, the islanders look upon it all with serenity, and hope that tourism won't go the way **18** of sugar.

Where to Go

In this section we examine separately each of the Canary Islands, its geography and personality, where to stay and what to see. We begin with the two principal islands, followed by the five less populous islands, from east to west.

Direction Finding: the Islands and their Capitals

Tenerife (Santa Cruz de Tenerife); The Everything Island
Gran Canaria (Las Palmas); Beaches and Bustle
Lanzarote (Arrecife); Black is Beautiful
Fuerteventura (Puerto del Rosario); Sahara-on-Sea
Gomera (San Sebastián); Columbus Slept Here
La Palma (Santa Cruz de la Palma); Paradise Found
El Hierro (Valverde); World's End.

From snowy Teide to Lanzarote's desert sand, the Canaries shatter preconceptions about volcanic isles.

Flowers flourish in La Orotava, old colonial town on Tenerife.

Teide retains its mystique: ever present, ever visible, it looms above one, awesomely.

The down-to-earth delights of Tenerife are as impressive. The flowers grow in wild profusion and in exotic varieties.

If you imagine that a volcanic island is a desert with grotesque rock formations and ruthlessly strewn chunks of cooled lava, you'll find just that in the south of the island. But you may be unprepared for the other side of Tenerife: mile after mile of green fields of bananas, tomatoes, potatoes; mountainsides of beech, eucalyptus and pine…a miraculous fertility achieved by irrigation—and centuries of hard work.

The coastline is as varied as the interior. You can take your pick from black sand, grey sand, golden sand, rocks, cliffs, tame beaches or wild capes.

If you prefer to turn your back on nature, you'll enjoy Tenerife's dignified old towns or eminently undignified discotheques. Whatever you're looking for you can find on this island. Everything, that is, except winter and haste.

Tenerife
Area: 790 sq. miles
Pop. 450,000

Largest of the Canaries in area if not in population, Tenerife is a whole world on one island. In the course of a day you can pick bananas, throw snowballs, swim in the Atlantic, climb mountains and go to the opera.

Tenerife's superlatives start at the top: Teide, highest mountain in all Spain, has awed travellers since ancient times. Even today, when you can soar nearly to the summit in a cable car, snow-topped

TENERIFE

Playa
de las Teresitas

San Andrés

1024 *Mirador*
Monte de ● *Pico del Inglés*
las Mercedes

La Laguna

**SANTA CRUZ
DE TENERIFE**

Bajamar

Las Caletillas

Aeropuerto
de los Rodeos

La Esperanza

Candelaria

Puerto de Güimar

N

Mesa del Mar

Tacoronte

La Victoria
de Acentejo

La Matanza
de Acentejo

Roque de Fasnia

Punta de Abona

0   5   10 km

0   3   6 miles

La Orotava

Parque Nacional

Fasnia

Punta del Camello

Puerto de la Cruz

Jardín
Botánico

2402

Granadilla
de Abona

El Médano

San Juan

San
Marcos

Las Cañadas

Vilaflor

Aeropuerto
Reina Sofía

Costa del Silencio

Garachico

Icod
de los Vinos

Pico del Teide
3718

Adeje

Palm-Mar

Faro de la Rasca

Punta de Buenavista

Santiago del Teide

Guía de Isora

Los Cristianos

Buenavista

Playa de
las Américas

*Punta
de Teno*

Los Gigantes
Puerto de
Santiago

San Juan

O C E A N O   A T L Á N T I C O

Santa Cruz de Tenerife
Pop. 200,000

Until the invention of the jet package tour, most visitors reached Tenerife via its sizeable port. The long, well-kept maritime promenade of Santa Cruz de Tenerife gives a fair idea of what's to come: palm trees, bright business-like buildings, a clamour of languages, a roar of new cars. All the traffic converges on the circular Plaza de España, in the middle of which stands an unusual tower in the form of a four-sided cross. The memorial to Civil War dead *(monumento a los caídos)* is a familiar landmark on the skyline.

Nearby are open-air cafés in or out of the hot sun, where you can relax and sniff the flavour of this city: a charming Spanish provincial capital true to style. A Government Tourist Office on the plaza offers free maps, brochures and answers to most of your questions. The main post office is here, too, as well as the **Archaeological Museum,** with important exhibits illustrating the life of the Guanches, the island's first inhabitants (see page 86).

Some visitors postpone cultural pursuits and plunge straight into the shopping. Due to comparatively low luxury taxes, prices are often very much lower than at home. To be sure of the best buys, shop around.

Conveniently for shoppers, the area extending uphill from the plaza is the island's banking centre. Most of the banks occupy straight-forward, ultra-modern buildings, but one on the Plaza de la Candelaria is different. It operates in a classic 18th-century Canaries building (restored in 1956). The soft clatter of calculating machines permeates the exquisite open patio surrounded by delicate woodwork. The building, now something of a national monument, is called the **Palacio Carta.** It was built in 1742 by order of Don Matías Bernardo Rodríguez Carta, general treasurer of the royal estate.

The capital's principal religious and historical monument is an easy walk from here. Look for the strange church tower, with its octagonal belfry; it might have been copied from a medieval Florentine drawing. This is the **Church of the Immaculate Conception** *(Iglesia Matriz de la Concepción)*, built at the beginning of the 16th century and partly rebuilt after a fire in the mid-17th century. Aside from its rich gilt statues, the church boasts several interesting historical relics—worth seeing if you can find them. Anonymously displayed behind glass is the original cross carried by the Spanish conquerors of Tenerife, as well as Nelson's faded battle flag, captured by local defenders at the battle of Santa Cruz de Tenerife on July 25, 1797 (see page 15).

Going down to the sea in minimum formality to exploit the winter sun.

Just behind the church lies the Barranco de Santos, one of the deep ravines characteristic of the Canaries, and a reminder of former volcanic upheavals. A few streets away from the bustling, modern centre of the city, goats graze in the *barranco,* oblivious to all the activity.

Morning is the best time to visit the so-called **African Market** known officially as El Mercado de Nuestra Señora de Africa. This clean, airy, native-style food market surrounds an ample, fountained patio. It amounts to a really super supermarket based on the age-old system of small competing stalls. Try some of the pastries and home-made cheeses, have a glance at the varieties of fish, fruit, vegetables and flowers—or buy a live chicken or a canary.

For a relaxing afternoon in Santa Cruz, stroll through García Sanabria Park (named after a popular mayor), and generally referred to as the Municipal Park. This cool sanctuary, famous for its floral clock, offers a unique assortment of tropical trees and flowers, as well as colourful birds and monkeys to add a final exotic touch.

The park borders the **Rambla del General Franco,** the city's most splendid avenue—brightened by leafy trees and impressive architecture, traditional and modern. The Rambla eventually converges with the Avenida de Anaga, the seafront boulevard. Heading out of town towards Las Teresitas, stop to look at the old artillery pieces guarding the **Castle of Paso Alto** *(Castillo de Paso Alto).* Among exhibits here is the elaborately engraved cannon which wounded Nelson at the battle of Tenerife in 1797.

Nine kilometres from Santa Cruz lies the beach of **Las Teresitas,** unique in its way, for it claims to be the largest artificial beach in the world. Golden sand, enough to cover an area about a mile long and 100 yards wide, was shipped here from the Sahara. On an island best known for black volcanic sand, Las Teresitas stands out like a peroxide blonde in darkest Africa. The small neighbouring fishing port of SAN ANDRÉS will never be the same again.

Puerto de la Cruz
Pop. 30,000

On the opposite side of the island, Puerto de la Cruz may be short on desirable sand beaches but gives holiday-makers everything else they could want, including an outstandingly mild climate. Something is always happening in Puerto de la Cruz, the island's principal tourist centre; whether it's a local band showing off, street artists hawking their wares, three camels named Pajarito, Laurito and Bonito swaying through the town with giggling tourists aloft, or fishermen coming home with pompano, ray and squid.

Puerto de la Cruz—often called just Puerto—first came to the notice of the world as the main port from which Canary Island wines were shipped to Europe.

Like Santa Cruz and other big cities of the archipelago, it is a paradise for shoppers of all ages and all tastes. Day and night, streams of window-shoppers stroll from the **seafront promenade** of Avenida de Colón into the side-streets and along towards the older centre of the town, lured by temptingly inexpensive embroidery, liquor, Toledo swords and jewellery, bikinis, dolls, wristwatches and shoes. Beside the local food market, on the seafront, there's an additional shopping enclave, reminiscent of a Middle-Eastern bazaar. Salesmen in tented stalls try to tempt you to buy jewellery, woodwork, seashells, stuffed alligators and kitsch knick-knacks.

Holiday Puerto de la Cruz—a cool, leisurely lunch beside the pool.

The **Church of the Rock of France** *(Iglesia de la Peña de Francia)* was completed around the end of the 17th century. Although the exterior has been redesigned, the large arched interior conforms to the pleasant Canary pattern. Note the elaborate 17th-century baroque retable, along with unusual polychrome wood sculptures.

Only a few streets away, the town's traditional **main square**—Plaza Charco—is a lively focal point for local and tourist life. The outdoor café,

under the great palm trees in the centre, stays busy day and night.

Just off the square, the **old town** of Puerto de la Cruz remains remarkably unchanged. Here are narrow streets with faded wooden balconies, carved doors and distinctive shutters behind which local women sit and embroider while spying on passersby. Towards noon they will go down to the small **fishing port** to buy the raw materials for lunch; there are no middlemen here. The black lava beach is too small for all the boats so they're parked like cars in the street above.

One of Puerto de la Cruz's most exclusive and historic hotels, the former Gran Hotel Taoro, which stood in its own private park on a hill overlooking the town and coast has been completely gutted and rebuilt into one of the most luxurious casinos in Europe, the **Casino Taoro**. In the neighbourhood are hotels, fashionable villas and all kind of institutions, reflecting the international character of Puerto de la Cruz: an English school, a British Library and an Anglican church used by many different nationalities and faiths.

The **plateau of La Paz,** a promontory overlooking Martiánez Beach, also has a foreign connection. It was owned by an Irishman named Bernard Walsh, who came to live in Tenerife in the early 18th century. Since the Spanish language has no letter "W" he changed his name to Valois; a local street is named after him. The simple white church of La Paz is an 18th-century reconstruction of a chapel begun in 1591.

La Paz—the name means "peace"—was probably so called after a conference on this very spot which brought an end to the bloody fighting between Conquistadors and Guanches, many of whom lived in the caves of the cliffs here. The **cliffside** is floodlit at night to give tourists yet another sight to remember.

Puerto's chief drawback—lack of a real beach with the real sea—has been turned now to its advantage with the installation of the **Lido,** an 8-acre recreational zone. Although a totally "artificial" creation, the Lido not only has magnificent facilities but the architecture is interesting, typically "Canarian" and harmonious, and the sea is ever-present.

Young visitors romp among roots and branches at Botanical Garden.

Flora

Tenerife's **Botanical Garden,** just outside Puerto de la Cruz, is a cool, green sanctuary so full of tropical vegetation that you expect to hear parrots cawing and monkeys chattering. The management has obliged with a small zoo. Countless additional birds fly in, voluntarily, to enjoy the scenery.

Officially called the Jardín de Aclimatación, this tourist showplace was founded by royal decree in 1788. There are lonesome palms of every variety, including one named *jipijapa;* its fibres go to make so-called Panama hats. In "cactus corner" a rather unnecessary notice warns, "Don't touch". A favourite with young visitors is a South American variety of fig tree, whose enormous branches and roots have become intertwined into one outlandish treehouse, that would have suited Tarzan.

But you don't have to go to the meticulously arranged Botanical Garden to see beautiful flora. Everywhere on Tenerife, the roadsides are fragrant with honeysuckle and mimosa; they blush with bougainvillaea, poinsettia and jacaranda. Glance into anybody's garden and you're more than likely to see a dazzlingly beautiful frangipani tree or a bed of *strelitzia,* the Bird-of-Paradise flowers.

Points North

La Laguna, the island's ecclesiastical and cultural capital, is a city well worth exploring. Walk through street after narrow street of distinguished old houses; sometimes a door left ajar will reveal an exemplary Canaries patio—a refuge of cool, green tranquillity.

The **cathedral,** with its huge vaulted ceiling, turns out to be a surprisingly modern structure in spite of its design. It was consecrated in 1913, more than 400 years after the city's founding. Artistic interest here centres on the late 16th-century Flemish altar panels.

The town's oldest church (1497), a few streets away, stands out by its curiously shaped, seven-storey-tall belfry and watchtower (1697). The **Church of the Immaculate Conception** *(Iglesia de la Concepción),* containing some fine wood carving, has been declared a national monument.

But this is not only a city of tradition, of old men in wide-brimmed black fedoras taking the early sunshine on park benches. It is also a centre of youth and learning—seat of the only full-scale university in the archipelago. The **University** of La Laguna has faculties of law, science philosophy, journalism, music, and so on.

Near the university's extended campus, by the main road, stands a modern statue of a local hero, the friar José de Anchieta, born in La Laguna in 1533. Sent as a missionary to Brazil, he is said to have converted two million Indians to Christianity. The statue was a gift from the people of Brazil.

BAJAMAR, a northern coastal resort under La Laguna's jurisdiction, is a growing tourist centre. To compensate for the lack of beaches—the sea is wild in this area—the ocean has been corralled into large artificial pools. At high tide the waves surge in, changing the water. At other times the pools are ideally calm for swimming.

After having passed the semi-tropical plateau around La Laguna, the road going north-east begins to climb into a zone of remarkably lush vegetation. The forest of **Monte de las Mercedes** is a cool, dark world of towering laurels, beech trees, pines and wild flowers. At the end of a serpentine road, there's a dizzying view from **Pico del Inglés** (Englishman's peak); just why the promontory is called "English" is anybody's guess. Glorious green valleys spread down to the sea. Two widely contrasting views can be observed from Pico del Inglés: looking due north you'll see Punta Hidalgo with its churning seas. Turn to face south and you'll make out the new, placid beach of Las Teresitas near Santa Cruz.

Tenerife's Centre

La Orotava, a city of stately houses and elegant little parks, is the centre of the strikingly beautiful Orotava Valley, some 24 square miles of green trees, flaming bushes and bright blue flowers. The German naturalist Alexander von Humboldt, on seeing the valley for the first time, is said to have fallen to his knees to thank God for such a marvel of creation.

The town is famous for its unbelievably beautiful "flower carpets" that originated here and that are to be seen each year at Corpus Christi.

La Orotava is eminently pleasant to stroll in despite its steep streets. Sightseeing from a bus or car you might miss parts of its bizarre skyline of towers, cupolas, turrets and unexpected protuberances. **30** The most interesting single

street is **Calle San Francisco,** with its many venerable façades—one house is dated 1590. Here are fine examples of the intricate woodwork characteristic of Canaries balconies, window-frames and doors.

The **Church of the Immaculate Conception** (*Nuestra Señora de la Concepción*), with its twin towers, baroque façade and Byzantine dome, has been declared a historic monument. It was begun in 1503 but wiped out by an earthquake two centuries later; the present church was consecrated in 1788. Inside, the elegant columns, the high altar of marble and alabaster and countless silver and gold treasures, compel admiration.

La Matanza and La Victoria de Acentejo, two towns near La Orotava, but towards the coast, are notable rather for their names and histories than for their present-day attractions.

La Matanza means "the massacre"—a morbid name for any town to bear. Blood flowed in quantity here in 1494 when invading Spanish troops were ambushed in a deep

In a classic Canaries patio, girls concentrate on delicate needlework.

Parasols and footprints in the sand show tourism's impact on Canaries.

only escaped by donning a plain soldier's uniform and running for his life.

Fernández de Lugo's revenge came a year and a half later and was known as the Second Battle of Acentejo. Near the same ravine, the Spaniards overwhelmed the natives, now weakened by fighting and by epidemics. A crude chapel was built on the site to celebrate the victory and around it sprang up the village named La Victoria. Within a matter of months the entire island of Tenerife was pacified, thereby bringing to a close almost a century of struggle for control of the Canary Islands.

TACORONTE, well known throughout the islands for its wines, is just a mile or two off the main road. This neat farming community is worth the small detour both for its own sake and for a much admired and venerated 17th-century figure of Christ. Known as the **Christ of the Sorrows** (*Cristo de los Dolores*), it stands in the local church and represents Jesus with a Cross in one hand, and with the other upon his heart.

After Los Rodeos Airport along the new modern motorway from Puerto de la Cruz to Santa Cruz, a second-

ravine. The defending Guanche forces, primitive though they may have been, pinned down the Conquistadors in a classic cowboy-and-Indian-style situation. Nine hundred of the invaders died here, and the Spanish commander, **32** Alonso Fernández de Lugo, ary road marked "La Esperanza" (hope) branches off to the right. This is the start of a long, increasingly picturesque drive down the centre of the island. It begins in the **forest of la Esperanza.**

Climbing through this forest of giant pines and eucalyptus trees, we see the most tangible evidence that, in the Canary Islands, flora is determined by altitude, not geography. A few hundred feet above sea level, vegetation suddenly changes: everything is green and fresh. The Canary pines do more than just beautify the countryside. They absorb moisture from the clouds and transmit it through their roots to the earth. Where there are pines there is no erosion.

In this rolling, climbing forest is a place where history was made: Las Raíces (the roots). Here, in June 1936, Francisco Franco—then captain-general of the Canary Islands—met with other army officers to plan what became the National Movement. Within a month he was on his way to lead the victorious forces in the Spanish Civil War. An obelisk in the forest, commemorating the meeting, is dedicated to the Caudillo.

As the road gains altitude, the temperature begins to fall, and the view becomes ever more spectacular. With distance and haze, the colours below darken; the glorious green of the Orotava Valley to the right fades into an indistinct grey.

Next comes **Las Cañadas National Park,** within the perimeter of one of the earth's largest volcanic craters. At this altitude in this grim terrain, scrub is the only sign of life. The road cuts through hills of stratified volcanic lava, black, grey, white and red.

Throughout this drive **Mount Teide** has been coming awesomely closer. Though Teide (it rhymes with lady) has been dormant since the end of the 17th century, hikers reaching the top can still smell the sulphur fumes. Climbing is no longer the only way up. A cable-car *(teleférico)* has been built virtually to the 12,000-foot summit. The 30-passenger cabins, suspended from a cable, pitch and toss all the way to the top in eight minutes flat. If the cabin or the altitude worries you, take comfort in the small statue of Jesus blessing the control centre right the way back at the bottom of the line.

When you reach the cable-car terminal the air is so thin you may not feel like tackling **33**

Top of the world: cable car lifts tourists to summit of Mount Teide.

the short hike to the summit. But even from the terminal you can admire the snow and a breathtaking all-round panorama.

Except for a government-run hotel, a TV transmitter and an observatory, man's presence on the mountain is limited. But so is nature's. This is fire-and-brimstone country, a lonely and desolate place where only a single species of bird flourishes—*el pájaro del Teide* (the Teide bird). And a curious blue violet is the only flower that's ever

been known to grow here.

But you'll soon cheer up with a few deep breaths of the purest air anywhere. All of the archipelago's inhabited islands are visible on a clear day, and it's tempting to pretend you can make out the coast of Africa.

On any continent anywhere, Spain's tallest mountain would be a worthwhile sight. Here, in the middle of the Atlantic Ocean, of all places, Teide is an incomparable experience on no account to be missed.

Round the Coast

Now a glance at some coastal highlights of Tenerife, heading clockwise from Santa Cruz:

Candelaria (23 kilometres from the capital on the southern motorway *[autopista]*) is a town with a narrow beach of black sand and a long, mystical history. Before Spaniards ever set foot on Tenerife, an image of the Virgin is said to have been washed ashore. Although they knew nothing of its Christian meaning, the primitive Guanches worshipped it. After the conquest the Spaniards built a small church dedicated to the image. The statue—and much of the church—was destroyed in a 19th-century disaster. An over-size **basilica** was then built, and a replica of the legendary madonna set up in it. The reconstituted statue of Our Lady of Candelaria, patron saint of the Canary Islands, is the object of numerous pilgrimages. Curiously enough, the complexion of the madonna and child in the replica is strongly reminiscent of the colour of volcanic rock.

Along the seafront near the church, don't miss the bizarre **statues** of idealized Guanches standing to attention all in a row with their backs to the Atlantic. These cavemen in animal skins, armed with clubs, are tall, handsome, bearded—and presumably blue-eyed and valiant. Nowhere else in the archipelago has the cult of the "noble savage" been carried so far.

By the time the road reaches the latitude of EL MÉDANO, the nature of the interior has changed; from lush green it has become parched. But the coastline is alluring—miles of fine, light sand caressed by gentle waves. Inevitably, this former charming fishing hamlet has grown into a tourist complex of hotels and villas. And with Tenerife's new transoceanic jet airport only a few miles beyond, the development seems destined to accelerate.

To the west of the new airport, in an area of rugged natural beauty, a resort called **La Costa del Silencio** (the silent coast) has been developed. Unlike the broad sand beaches of El Médano, the coast here is rocky, with natural and man-made steps leading down to unspoilt coves. As the name indicates, this is not the place for swingers or people who enjoy crowds; but it can offer sun, sea and serenity in plenty.

Just around the tip of the island and turning north-west, a major tourist complex has been developed on the edge of *malpaís* (badlands)—a scrub-covered lava wilderness. Once a small fishing port with a deserted beach, LOS CRISTIANOS has evolved into a Mediterranean-style resort. In the main street, a pedestrians-only thoroughfare, all the cafés and restaurants have tables down the centre where visitors can enjoy refreshments and watch passers-by. The port is full of pleasure craft; small boats, three-masters and cruisers can be hired for a day of deep-sea fishing or sailing along the coast. And if the pace of resort-life becomes too hectic you can always stagger down to the harbour and board the boat to the escape island of Gomera (see page 62).

To the north-west of LOS Cristianos is PLAYA DE LAS AMÉRICAS, a new town which has been developed as a complete holiday centre. Year-round temperatures here average a degree or two higher than in the north of the island.

Also on the west coast, and coming up quickly in the popularity stakes, is LOS GIGANTES, a tastefully planned resort in the "grand" tradition.

West from 'Puerto'

Two outstanding sights may be covered in a half-day outing to the west of Puerto de la Cruz, along Tenerife's north coast.

In the heart of banana plantations and vineyards, sleepy ICOD DE LOS VINOS clusters round a carefully tended park created to honour a very special tree. It's the most impressive surviving example of a plant which has intrigued people for ages, a **Dragon tree,** a botanical freak like a fossil come to life. The tall, broad specimen in Icod is said to be 3,000 years old. It looks its age. Birds flit among its maze of branches, and photographers try to capture the knife-blade contours of its green leaves. On a quiet day, waiting for the next coachload of tourists to arrive, one can sit in the shade of this other-worldly relic and understand how the ancients came to believe it was imbued with magic powers.

Finally, GARACHICO. Your impressions as you look down on this town from the road high above will depend on your temperament. A pessimist may recall with a shudder the volcano which spewed molten horror on Garachico in the 18th century, wiping out modest **peninsula** created by the eruption itself. One important landmark which survived the catastrophe of Garachico is the **Castle of San Miguel** (*Castillo de San Miguel*), a 16th-century fortress. A few other buildings still bear the arms of the noblemen who dwelt in the town before Mount Bermeja erupted. A melancholy reminder of disaster, or an inspiring example of human perseverance? The choice depends on you.

Canaries

You don't have to be an expert—or a canary—to tell the difference between a male and a female canary.

Only the males know how to sing.

Canaries, the most famous wildlife found in the islands, take their name from the archipelago, and not vice-versa. They are also found on Madeira and the Azores.

Serinus canaria was first imported to Europe in the 16th century. Originally they were colourless birds, but breeders in Europe were able to develop a yellow variety. Other festive colours followed.

If a tree lived to be 3,000 it would look like Dragon of Icod.

its profitable port, most of the buildings, and hundreds of the inhabitants. The optimist, standing safely in the path of the now-petrified lava, may smile at the sight of a carefully planned new town with neat houses and productive fields jutting out into the sea on the

37

Gran Canaria

Area: 592 sq. miles
Pop. 600,000

In spite of its name, Gran Canaria is only the third biggest of the Canaries. But it's second to none for its perfect beaches and sophisticated night-life, for its history and hubbub, off-beat sightseeing and shopping.

Almost circular in shape, Gran Canaria is about the size of the Shetland Islands or slightly smaller than Guadeloupe—small enough to get to know, yet large enough for the climate to change radically with latitude or altitude. If it's overcast and chilly in Las Palmas at one end, it's probably hot and clear at Maspalomas at the other. If you need a break from sunbathing, you

can take to the hills for soft, cool breezes.

The coastline ranges from awe-inspiring cliffs to golden dunes. Inland you can choose between stark mountains and tranquil valleys. The contrast of life-styles is just as total. Travelling from the boisterous capital to one of the languorous provincial villages is like abandoning Miami Beach for the Everglades.

Apart from its ever-expanding tourism, Gran Canaria earns its living from agriculture. Under intensive cultivation, the soil produces year-round crops of bananas, tomatoes and potatoes to satisfy the cravings of less temperate zones. Local achievements in wines and liqueurs are also worth investigating at first hand.

Island attractions extend beyond beaches to lively shopping streets.

Las Palmas
Pop. 350,000

Bustling Las Palmas is more than just a provincial capital. As the largest city in the Canaries, it's a major commercial and historical centre, a cosmopolitan resort and a vital seaport all rolled into one.

You can begin to understand Las Palmas in **Puerto de la Luz** (port of light), the cap-ital's dockside area. Along the docks or anchored just off-shore awaiting a berth you can see ships from all imaginable seafaring nations, sailing under familiar or bizarre flags. Side by side lie Chinese freighters and Russian trawlers, Spanish mail boats, Lebanese tankers, Japanese fish canning ships and Greek freighters. The huge modern harbour is host to proud liners as it is to rusted tramp steamers. More than a thousand ships a month arrive to take on fuel or unload cargo or just give the crew a break. In impeccable uniforms or the most haphazard of outfits, sailors of the world fan out from Puerto de la Luz to gaze wistfully at the **39** girls and the shop windows, to promenade, have a sun-bath, eat and drink, live it up... in fact, to do just about everything the other tourists do!

Just across the street from the Santa Catalina pier where pleasure and fishing craft are moored, you can't miss the social hub of Las Palmas. **Santa Catalina Park** is essentially a gigantic outdoor café, humming day and night with most of the "real" languages of the world, helped now and then by pidgin English and phrase-book Spanish. Here the sailors swig beer, lavishly gowned visitors from nearby West Africa sip tea, and tourists with peeling noses down excesses of bargain-priced whisky and gin. Here, too, are the tough, tanned oil-rig men who work off the African coast but call Las Palmas home. You'll also see Canarians and mainland Spaniards talking energetically while nursing coffee or brandy and contemplating this undeniably exotic scene. If you can't forget the cares of the world, you can catch up on the news at the kiosks here; they sell all the leading European newspapers and magazines. Here, too, you'll be tempted with imaginative varieties of tourist knick-knacks as well as the inexpensive free-trade goods for which the Canaries are renowned (see page 87).

A short walk through the dust and exhaust fumes of the central shopping district leads to **Las Canteras,** on the opposite side of the peninsula to Puerto de la Luz: $2\frac{1}{2}$ miles of fine sand—a beautiful beach by any standards. Not even

LAS PALMAS DE GRAN CANARIA

Mid-Atlantic metropolis: city of Las Palmas surrounds its harbour.

the occasional grotesque building, tawdry bazaar or high-powered salesman can spoil the mood. Soak up the sun here and think of the rest of the world shivering at home. Dip a toe in the mighty Atlantic Ocean. It couldn't be calmer, thanks to a natural barrier reef about 200 yards offshore. Yet this is one of the very few Canaries beaches manned by lifeguards, equipped with observation towers, two-way radios and motorboats.

Cheap, frequent buses link Las Canteras and the port area with the rest of Las Palmas, sprawling to the south. In your explorations you may be disorientated by the sight of an-

other city beach. It's Las Al-caravaneras, back to back with Las Canteras, its much more glamorous competitor. Because of the increasing concentration of shipping just offshore, activities on Las Al-caravaneras are now limited to sunbathing or football-playing rather than swimming.

round. Doramas Park, a city park named after one of the Guanche kings, is particularly well landscaped. Among several other wonders within the park is a luxury hotel in classic

Columbus attended mass in church at rear, in Vegueta, Las Palmas.

Ciudad Jardín (Garden City) shows how the "other half" lives. Whether the houses are palatial or relative-ly modest, the gardens around them sing with colour all year

Canaries style. Here, too, is the **Pueblo Canario** (Canary Village), an attempt to pull together all the threads of Canaries folklore specifically for the tourist public. Despite a slightly forced atmosphere of gaiety, holiday-makers hap-pily flock here for *sangría,* folk-dancing displays, handicraft shopping and sunshine.

The man who designed the architectural ensemble of the Pueblo Canario was Néstor de la Torre (1887–1938), a local artist and designer, commemorated in the Néstor Museum, facing the main square of the "village" (see MUSEUMS, page 86).

A more celebrated artistic figure from Las Palmas was Benito Pérez Galdós (1843–1920), one of Spain's great and most prolific writers. The author of scores of books in series entitled *Episodios nacionales* (National Episodes) and *Novelas contemporáneas* (Contemporary Novels), he is best known for his pitiless exposure of Spain's 19th-century social problems. The house where he was born (at 6, Calle Cano) is now a museum. The nearby opera house, named after him, is the unchallenged centre of the island's musical and cultural life. Néstor de la Torre contributed bright, cheerful decorations to the old-fashioned **Teatro Pérez Galdós.**

The theatre faces the Barranco (ravine) de Guiniguada. The Spanish conquerors and native Guanches fought many battles in this gorge, now the path of an *autopista* (motorway). On the far side of the Guiniguada begins the oldest part of Las Palmas—the *barrio* of **Vegueta,** where the Spanish forces first set up camp in 1478. History lurks behind every wall.

The hermitage of San Antonio Abad is a modest old church rebuilt two centuries ago on the ruins of the island's very first church. A plaque on the façade tells us that Columbus prayed here in the memorable year of 1492.

Much more Columbiana occupies the building now called **Columbus's house** *(Casa de Colón)*. This elegant house, built around a charming patio, was the residence of the island's first governor, Pedro de Vera (appointed in 1482). Columbus stayed here in 1492 and again on his triumphant return in 1493 and in 1502. Now a museum, the house recreates the age of discovery in exhibitions of navigational instruments, charts, weapons and everyday items of the late 15th century. On the same premises are the provincial fine arts museum and historical archives (see page 86).

Only five years after Columbus's first voyage, work began on a new cathedral for Las Palmas, just around the corner from the governor's residence. It remains unfinished to this 43

day. Built out of local stone, a mixture of Gothic and neo-Classic styles, **St. Anne's Cathedral** *(Catedral de Santa Ana)* rises sombrely over the old town. For a few pesetas you can see the treasury, with exhibits of ancient art and jewellery.

Facing the cathedral are several unusual black stone statues of dogs representing the aboriginal dogs after whom the Canary Islands are said to be named. The sculptor must have been undecided as to whether they were mastiffs, dobermans or boxers.

St. Anne's Square *(Plaza de Santa Ana)* is where the religious processions of Las Palmas begin or end. On certain holidays the plaza is covered with flowers arranged on the ground in intricate designs. These floral carpets transform the normally quiet square into the vibrant heart of the island.

Southern Exposure

The main road south from Las Palmas with its considerable traffic is not quite the scenic route the maps would have us believe. Apart from a few pleasant ocean views, there's mile after mile of desolate countryside to contemplate.

Fortunately, it's a motorway (expressway) all the way to San Agustín.

Soon a romantic, rugged mountain range rises in the distance like a Western film set, and, sure enough, many a low-budget cowboy film has, in fact, been shot here.

And then, out of nowhere, looms the overwhelming tourist complex of **Playa del Inglés** (Englishman's beach), some kind of reincarnation of Miami Beach in mid-Atlantic. From San Agustín past Playa del Inglés up to the landmark of the Maspalomas lighthouse stretch 10 miles of golden sand beaches backed by a new kind of boom-town sprawl. Tall hotels, squat bungalows, blocks of flats, hamburger stands, swimming pools, real estate offices and shopping centres proliferate. The Casino Gran Canaria in Hotel Tamarindos is a landmark. Shop and restaurant signs abound in usually imperfect German, Swedish, English, Finnish, French and, occasionally, Spanish. Obviously, this is where it's all happening.

Maspalomas dunes, Gran Canaria: endless sand and sea for everyone.

Fishermen, watched by local children, sort out their day's catch.

Though the developers and their landscaping contractors have worked hard to tame and groom the surrounding countryside, you can never quite shake off that desert feeling. The **dunes of Maspalomas** are large enough, and unspoiled enough, to constitute a local mini-Sahara of great beauty. An oasis nearby relieves the blinding effect of seemingly endless white sand.

Round the coast beyond Maspalomas smaller developments—*urbanizaciones* is the bald but accurate Spanish term— have been built or are being planned for just about every promising cove. Outstanding among them are PATALAVACA and ARGUINEGUÍN, with their limpid waters and 350 days of sunshine a year, and the tourist complex called PUERTO RICO, built around a garden and a developing marina.

The coast road comes to an end opposite Las Palmas on the far side of the island, for the terrain is too rugged here. The last town is PUERTO DE MOGÁN, a fishing village pinned to a mountainside plunging down to the sea.

To make a complete circuit of the island you have to continue inland—a rewarding if exhausting experience over harrowing mountain roads.

Northern Coastal Zone

The northern coastal zone of Gran Canaria is where the bananas come from. Millions of them. Green terraced plantations slope gently down from the mountains to the edge of the sea.

Bananaland's capital is **Arucas,** an agreeable white town overshadowed by an immense neo-Gothic **cathedral.** This titanic, stained-glass building, a 20th-century creation, is as surprising as the sight of the Eiffel Tower would be here among the plantations. The rest of the town is a hilly delight.

The inland road westwards from Arucas follows a breathtaking route through the mountains, past many **caves** big enough to live in. A few of them are actually still inhabited, serviced with running water and electricity.

Finally, near the coast, we reach the **Convent of Valerón** *(Cenobio de Valerón)*, a complex of hundreds of small caves cut into a steep mountainside. It is said to have been a sort of primitive pagan convent. According to island lore, the daughters of aboriginal noble families spent their youth in these small cells serving the native gods. At the age of 35 they were finally allowed to choose marriage or remain in the sanctuary for life.

Other Guanche memories are associated with the city of GALDAR, once a royal capital of the aborigines. The palace of the *Guanarteme,* the native chieftain, was destroyed in the 17th century, but some Guanche relics are preserved in the town hall. Near the city of Galdar is the mountain of the same name, very similar in outline to Tenerife's Mount Teide. From certain vantage points—along the beach at Las Canteras in Las Palmas, for instance—the two peaks appear confusingly paired on the horizon. But Galdar, though very much closer, is infinitely smaller than its apparent twin.

The town of AGAETE, to the south-west, is only about a kilometre from the sea. Its port, called **Puerto de las**

Bunches of bananas grow "upside down" on extensive plantation.

Nieves, is a haven of gentleness among the formidable cliffs making up this stretch of coast. It has a black volcanic beach and an elaborate harbour for a small fishing fleet.

Amongst the nearby rocks jutting out into the Atlantic, one formation is much taller and more commanding than the rest: it is known as the **Finger of God** *(El dedo de Dios)*.

Central Sights

Excursions to the centre of Gran Canaria usually include a leisurely halt in the peaceful valley town of **Teror** (no connection with the word *terror*, meaning dread). The old white-washed houses, often built around graceful patios, have traditional, carved balconies. The major landmark here is a large, typically Canarian church called the **Basilica of Our Lady of the Pine** (*Nuestra Señora del Pino*), that commemorates the miraculous discovery in 1481—in the branches of a pine tree—of a sacred effigy. The **Blessed Virgin of Teror** is the patron saint of the island of Gran Canaria.

On January 17, 1975, the richly robed, bejewelled and crowned statue of Madonna and Child was the target for one of the most sensational (and professional) crimes in Canaries history. Burglars broke through the 200-year-old ceiling of the church and methodically removed the most important diamonds, sapphires, gold and silver adornments. They left behind many items considered less valuable—or impossible to dispose of. Estimates on the value of the haul range from 10 to 20 million pesetas.

For a small charge you can enter the treasury of the church and see the statue of the patron saint on her silver throne at close quarters. Buy a pre-robbery picture postcard from the custodian, and you will be able to see just how much jewellery was taken.

The mountainous centre of the island makes for very tiring driving but gratifying sightseeing—panoramas of pine forests and almond groves, gnarled mountains and sheer cliffs. The best vantage point is at the **Cross of Tejeda** (*Cruz de Tejeda*), a monument at the top of the island's road system, at an altitude of about 4,800 feet. Originally a pine crucifix had been erected here, but harsh weather prompted its replacement by a cross of island stone. From here you have a first-rate view of the mysterious **Roque Nublo,** a natural rock formation standing like a statue on the horizon. The Guan-

Some sunbathers abandon sand for rocky grandeur elsewhere on coast.

49

ches are said to have worshipped it.

A *parador* (state-run hotel) has been built at Cruz de Tejeda. It's an ideal hideout if you yearn for isolation and pure mountain air—a model of rustic elegance many miles from the nearest commercial hotel. The village of TEJEDA, two miles away, is famous for its almond blossoms in February.

A much less remote location for a quiet stay is SANTA BRÍGIDA, an attractive town on the way back to Las Palmas. Because the microclimate here is exceptionally gentle, many Canarians and permanent foreign residents have built homes in these hills. The gardens around their villas are magnificent.

One of Gran Canaria's memorable natural features is **Bandama Crater,** an extinct volcano almost two-thirds of a mile across. Here for a change is a crater lacking in sinister undertones, for the interior of the cone, an almost perfect circle, is both green and fertile. Farm buildings nestling at the bottom, some 650 feet down, show just how tame the volcano is considered to be; the whole scene looks as cosy as a sleepy Swiss valley. All of this—as well as a sweeping view of about half the is-

land—may be seen from the vantage point at the top end of a spiralling road. The inevitable souvenir shop awaits the excursion coaches.

A final sight to see: Gran Canaria's second city, TELDE (not to be confused with Teide, Tenerife's majestic mountain). Telde was the capital of Doramas, the legendary Guanche chieftain who fought off the Spanish invaders in 1478. Now it is a stately colonial city of genteel houses with fine pine balconies. The twin-turreted **Church of St. John** *(Iglesia de San Juan),* dating from the late 15th century, is considered the oldest church on Gran Canaria. Its intricate, gilded wooden altarpiece is a splendid example of Flemish carving of that period. The Christ of the high altar is less an artistic triumph than a historical and physical curiosity. It is said to have been made by Indians in Mexico in the 16th century, using a secret process converting crushed maize-stalks into a durable construction material. Although the **statue** is more than life-sized, it weighs only about 15 pounds. This link with the New World is one of the ever-present reminders of the Canaries' role as a bridge over the Atlantic.

Lanzarote

Area: 310 sq. miles
Pop. 50,000

Lanzarote represents man's triumph over a hostile environment—a pockmarked lunar surface with over 300 volcanoes. Yet onions, potatoes, tomatoes, melons and grapes spring in abundance from the arid black volcanic ash. The scene startles and warms the heart. On Lanzarote, black is beautiful.

Even the island's name breeds legends. Does it honour a Genoese sailor by the name of Lancelotto, who stopped by in 1312? Or a French nobleman named Lancelot who accompanied the first settlers nearly a century later? Or could it be that in 1404, after pacifying the islanders, the Norman knight Jean de Béthencourt celebrated by breaking his lance, throwing the pieces into the air, and actually crying *"Lanza rota!"* (broken lance)? Whatever the story, Lanzarote, the Canary island closest to Europe, was the first to be conquered.

ARRECIFE (pop. 20,000), the principal port and latter-day capital, is a town of modest attractions. Passengers arriving by sea discover them even later than airborne tourists, for ships berth at a remote harbour on the far side of a fish canning area. The town harbour itself is too shallow to handle anything but fishing and pleasure craft. (*Arrecife* means "reef" in Spanish.)

The distant deep-water port is watched over by the **Fortress of San José** (*Fortaleza de San José*), while the fishing port, has its own fortress, **San Gabriel.** Now that pirate attacks are less likely, San Gabriel's stony hulk houses a small archaeological museum.

The attractive modern sea- **51**

Daily miracle of Lanzarote: crops sprout from black volcanic cinders.

front gardens are of fairly recent date and brighten the sleepy scene with their leafy trees, colourful flowers and a few patches of lawn. The secret is the municipal tank truck which waters the garden every eighth day. Water is too precious a commodity to be used more lavishly, even in this token display.

With rain so rare, and underground sources extremely limited, you may wonder how Lanzarote manages to be an agricultural island. Inland from Arrecife, fruit and vege-tables grow along graceful fur-rows of undulating volcanic ash. The black topsoil is the secret, discovered by the farm-ers in their adversity. These porous volcanic cinders, use-less in themselves, act as a sponge for the moisture of the night air, obtaining water for the plants and eliminating the need for rain. Perhaps the most unusual sight is the Lan-zarote version of **vineyards.** Each vine is set in its own mini-crater, protected from wind and excess sun by a low semi-circular wall of lava stones. The abstract patterns thus formed are almost hypnotic.

But these lovely farmlands contrast sharply with the raw remains of volcanic catastrophe, the broad "badlands" called *malpaís*, desolate plains above which volcanic hills of different hues and contours tower majestically.

Tourists climb one such mountain with perhaps unseemly gaiety. A camel ride up and down the **Fire Mountains** (*Montañas de Fuego*) as these hills are known, takes about 45 minutes. Even then the tourist has little time to ponder the profundities of the lunar landscape as seen from

the swaying hump of a camel. It's hard to tell who suffers most—the tourist or the camel.

More than a hundred of these animals are employed on the tourist beat, but many more are used for work on the land.

Geology and surrealist art coincide in desolate canyon on Lanzarote.

Volcanoes

If you'd like something to worry about, here's the track record on Canaries volcanoes—just a few of the bigger bangs:

1604 – Tenerife
1605 – Tenerife
1704/5 – Tenerife
1706 – Tenerife
1730 – Lanzarote
1798 – Tenerife
1824 – Lanzarote
1909 – Tenerife
1949 – La Palma island
1971 – La Palma island

Purists will note that these sure-footed landrovers are single-humped dromedaries, but everyone on Lanzarote calls them camels.

All guided tours of Lanzarote include a camel trip. The entire area has been turned into a sort of national park of desolation. The rugged black terrain is just the way one expects the world will look after it's all over.

As if to compensate for the Doomsday atmosphere, the guides wear gay pink uniforms as they demonstrate that fires still glow in the volcanic furnace beneath our feet. Cinders scooped up from a few inches beneath the surface turn out to be too hot to handle. A bit deeper and kindling-wood catches fire spontaneously. Another devilish experiment: the demonstrator pours water down a tube into the earth. A split second later steam hisses high into the air, a do-it-yourself geyser. A cheerful, modern bar-restaurant nearby uses devils and frying-pans as its trademarks. The food is cooked over this underground source of heat. The fuel is timeless, limitless and... free.

It's hard to imagine a country where the tourist itineraries take in the salt mines. But admiring excursionists do stop

to see the **salt flats of Janubio** (*Salinas de Janubio*) on the west coast of Lanzarote. The dazzling white of the drying salt set against the dramatic blue of the sea contrasts sharply with the black volcanic backdrop. Incidentally, the salt company provides the raw materials for a unique artistic event. For the festival of Corpus Christi, every spring, local artists pour salt dyed in various colours onto the streets of Arrecife to create religious and secular designs. It's an ephemeral exhibition, for once the festival is over, traffic soon scatters the salt carpets to the winds.

Hissing steam confirms volcanic activity on Lanzarote. Elsewhere, contentment glows in rural faces.

Another west-coast attraction, **El Golfo,** just up from Janubio, is an emerald-green lagoon beneath a cliffside resembling a gigantic petrified tidal wave about to break. This is the inner rim of a volcanic cone, half of which has disappeared beneath the sea. The strata, colours and mad whirls are fascinating. So is the contrast between the tranquil pool and the mighty ocean right next to it.

Yet another aquatic phenomenon lures visitors to the north-east coast of the island. **Jameos del Agua** is a grotto, open at both ends, with a small source of natural light from above. Shimmering effects transform the still water of this transparent pool in which thrives a species of small white spider-crab said to be found nowhere else in the world. Mood music and tropical landscaping have been introduced, without spoiling the sense of mystery and poetry; the artificial décor here, as at the Fire Mountains and elsewhere on the island, bears the trademark of the talented

César Manrique, Lanzarote's unofficial cultural mandarin.

The nearby cave of **Los Verdes** is sometimes spooky, sometimes inspiring. Four miles long, it stretches from a volcano through into the sea; the tunnel was blasted through the earth under the effect of exploding lava. A 50-minute guided tour over 1¼ miles includes an explanation of some of the legends, plus *son et lumière*. It will certainly appeal to all cave-lovers and vulcanophiles.

Off the north coast of Lanzarote, a little-known yet inhabited Canary island may be visited in a full-day outing. LA GRACIOSA is home for several hundred people, almost entirely fishermen. The beaches are excellent. There's no easy way to get there; it's about 40 minutes by motor launch from the tiny port of Orzola. Arrangements must be made in advance, subject to the state of the sea. Jean de Béthencourt anchored at La Graciosa before undertaking his protracted fight for the Canaries.

However, if it's swimming you're after, you need go no farther than PUERTO DEL CARMEN, a mere 10-minute drive from Lanzarote Airport. Puerto del Carmen is the new title for a village which used to

be known by the less alluring name of La Tiñosa (stained beach). The fishing town itself is so unspoiled that it's more romantic when seen from afar. But the area has become the major tourist resort of the island, with hotels, bungalow villages and a shopping centre. The genuine attraction here is as much beach as anyone could ask for, sloping into a calm blue sea.

Puerto del Carmen, the former "stained" beach, has recently been dubbed PLAYA BLANCA (white beach) by commercial interests. This public relations inspiration causes confusion, because there is another Playa Blanca, the original, about 35 kilometres south-west of Arrecife. You'll know you've stumbled upon Playa Blanca I if you see topless or bottomless sunbathers on the small, attractive beach. Though frowned upon by the authorities, nudism is concentrated on the southern tip of the island. Occasional arrests are intended to remind everyone of the official attitude, but there are not enough police to provide blanket enforcement.

Swimming obviously is a prime attraction of Lanzarote, but don't neglect the charming inland villages with their squat

Playa Blanca, Lanzarote: not far from paradise, say beach-lovers.

whitewashed houses and flower-gardens. The hamlets have names which sound strange even to Spanish or Canary ears—Soo and Uga and even Ye. Many indicate their Guanche origins by the initial letter "T"—Tinajo, Tahiche, Teseguite, Tao and the former capital, Teguise.

TEGUISE gives every appearance of being a town that history passed by. Its streets are pleasant but strangely quiet. Statues of lions inexplicably guard the modern town square. An improbable fortress atop an extinct volcano broods over the town. It's **St. Barbara's fortress** *(Fortaleza de Santa Bárbara)*, dating from the 14th century but repeatedly destroyed and rebuilt in later centuries. Nowadays Teguise's claim to fame lies in the manufacture of *timples*—the small stringed instruments (similar to ukuleles) used in Canaries folk music.

Exhibitions of folklore are the easiest way to see the distinctive Lanzarote costumes. However, just keeping your eyes open in the countryside **57**

FUERTEVENTURA

Isla de los Lobos

Corralejo

El Cotillo

La Oliva

Puerto del Rosario

Tetir   Playa
Blanca
El Puertito de   Aeropuerto
los Molinos
Casillas del Angel

Betancuria   La Antigua

Pozo
Negro

Tuineje

Pájara

Gran
Tarajal

Tarajalejo

La Jalita

Playa de
Barlovento   *Playa de*
Sotavento

Punta del Matorral
Morro de Jable

Punta de Jandía

0		10 km
0		10 miles

will give you the basic
idea—men in black hats and
women with heads almost
completely wrapped in a kind
of headscarf, topped by a
straw *sombrero* not unlike an
oriental coolie's hat. The wis-
dom of covering the hair, ears
and neck soon becomes evi-
dent; it's almost always windy
on Lanzarote, and the dust
blows hard.

Fuerteventura

Area: 780 sq. miles
Pop. 25,000

Beaches on Fuerteventura still
outnumber hotels. From the
air the island would appear to
be nothing but an outsize sand
dune emerging from the sea.
Less than 60 miles off the coast
of Africa, it has been likened
to a mini-Sahara—except that
the climate here is somewhat
kinder.

Only when the charter
flights from northern Europe
cruise in to the cheerful new jet
airport on the east coast does
the island snap momentarily
out of its sun-crushed lethar-
gy. But as the holiday-makers
themselves become attuned to
the unhurried local way of life,
the excitement subsides, and
the old women in black go
back to their desultory gossip.

For locals or visitors this is not the place to seek excitement; for a strictly lazy holiday by the sea, on the other hand, it's probably ideal.

PUERTO DEL ROSARIO, with a population of over 11,000, is the island's capital and main port. It used to be called Puerto Cabra (port of the goat) in recognition of the herds of goats but local promoters thought the name would not go down well with the tourists. In spite of the name change, the place remains a frontier town of extremely limited glamour—the kind of town which can't support a shoeshine boy (it's too dusty anyway).

But to be fair, the town, with its plucky little municipal park no bigger than a traffic island, makes no claim to be a point of great touristic interest. The lure here is white sand and blue sea; the rest just doesn't matter.

Only a kilometre or two down the coast, between Puerto del Rosario and the airport, is the easiest-to-reach beach, called PLAYA BLANCA. On any other resort island it would be considered outstanding, but the competition on Fuerteventura is much stronger. A government-run *parador* (state-run tourist hotel) at the southern end of Playa Blanca is as tasteful as these hotels usually are.

On the north coast, **Corralejo** was just a small fishing port until somebody had the sense to notice all the sand dunes in the neighbourhood. Nature has bleached the sand here to the colour of a brochure photographer's dream. A tourist boom is well under way, thanks to this exquisite sand and the bluest of blue seas. One top hotel has raised the stakes by inaugurating a huge fresh-water swimming pool—the ultimate in extravagant luxury on this parched, waterless island. A resident staff of camels and donkeys await the guests' pleasure in the hotel grounds.

Only 2 miles offshore is **Lobos Island,** with its fishing village and beaches even more secluded than on the "mainland" of Fuerteventura. The fishing here—from a boat or with snorkel and harpoon—is said to be the best in the Canaries. The professionals don't mind competition from tourists, since there are enough big fish to go round.

About halfway between Puerto del Rosario and Corralejo, on the main north-south road, is the town of LA OLIVA, with a solid fortress of **59**

Height of luxury: hotel pool beside a perfect beach of Fuerteventura.

a church. A few hundred yards off the road stands the so-called **House of the Colonels** *(Casa de los Coroneles)*, half-concealed up a rough and unmarked track. This decaying 18th-century building, once a colonial administrative headquarters, still exudes a certain haughty, if melancholy, Span-ish grandeur, despite the chickens and goats all around and an implausible Fuji-shaped hill in the background.

Nowhere on the island is history evoked more strikingly than in the town of **Betancuria** (named after the conqueror Jean de Béthencourt). Because of its theoretical invulnerability in the mountains in the centre of the island, Betancuria was made Fuerteventura's first capital at the beginning of the 15th century. It was also the episcopal seat of the entire Canary archipelago. But the strategists failed to reckon with the intrepid Berber pirates. In 1539 they not only overcame the mountains (it's a difficult enough drive today) but destroyed Betancuria's cathedral out of sheer spite. The **Church of St. Mary** *(Iglesia de Santa María)*, rebuilt in the early 17th century on an uncommonly grand scale, must be seen. In fact, the entire town of Betancuria, with its small white houses set among palms and stunted eucalyptus, is one of the most characteristic attractions of the island. Your first impression may well be that the town is as deserted as the House of the Colonels. But listen. Eventually you'll hear a baby wail or an old man cough, proving that life does go on, behind the shutters of this stately ancient capital.

The original primitive inhabitants of Fuerteventura were called Majoreros. Their stone-age antecedents, of the Cro-Magnon family, are the subject of many heroic tales. Today's islanders proudly refer to themselves as Majoreros.

In ancient times Fuerteventura was called Herbania because of its lush vegetation. Today's visitors find this too far-fetched to believe. But before the "civilizing" invaders from Europe depleted the pasturelands by importing too much livestock, Fuerteventura had really been fertile. On this island, erosion and drought, a vicious circle, followed the Spanish flag.

Occasional oases do exist amid the arid mountain ranges. There are clumps of palm trees, tomato groves, potato patches and the reassuring sight of whirling windmills. They come in the traditional, almost Dutch, style or in new aluminium models, made in USA. But it's largely a harsh, arid land where even the cactus looks as if it needs to be watered. Goats are the mainstay of agriculture, and the local goat's cheese is highly rated.

The road south from Puerto del Rosario eventually hits the coast at GRAN TARAJAL, the pompously named second port of the island. A large development is underway here, to exploit its underemployed crescent of beach. But more enterprising development schemes are afoot further to the south-west.

In the days of the Majoreros, the island was divided into two kingdoms. The smaller, more southerly realm was called **Jandía,** which is the present-day name for the peninsula at the foot stretching towards Gran Canaria. Along both sides of the peninsula are more miles of delightful, virgin beach than you'll find anywhere else in the archipelago. According to unconfirmed Canaries lore, German submarine crews used to sneak ashore here during World War II for rest and recreation. Nowadays the tourists arrive somewhat more conventionally—but the lure's the same: privacy, sun and sand.

The planners see it as Fuerteventura's answer to Maspalomas, only more exclusive. But they'll have to overcome all the problems of road-building and water supply before they really have the island in hand.

The Great Canaries Bug Bubble

Cactus is grown on all the Canary Islands, but not for its flowers. The variety known as *opuntia* harbours the cochineal insect, a pest which turned out to be a blessing in disguise. For the tiny bodies of the female bugs contain a dark-red liquid which makes a perfect natural dye.

In the 19th century, commercial enthusiasm for this bright colouring agent produced a Canaries boom. Billions of bugs gave their lives every year, dying for dyeing. Euphoria and prosperity (except among the bugs) reigned supreme.

But the crimson bubble burst within 50 years, when much cheaper chemical dyes were devised.

The industry did continue on a small scale, however, for cochineal is still required for certain cosmetics and food colouring. Expansion is now again underway, as new scientific uses have been found for the dye.

Gomera

Area: 146 sq. miles
Pop. 25,000

Of all the "Fortunate Isles", Gomera may be the luckiest. It's the only Canary island lacking a commercial airport. Mass tourism and other outside influences are consequently negligible. Gomera remains unaffected and authentic, a Shangri-La of steep, green terraced hills, smiling inhabitants and tranquillity.

The altitude of Gomera's highest peak, Alto de Garajonay, is 4,878 feet—no great height by Canaries standards—and yet the island often gives the impression of a fearsome maze of eerie crags. One hilltop may be within waving distance of the next, but driving between them on the principal highway is a dizzying ordeal of twists, turns and surprises. In this world of irreversible progress, you may be relieved to find the main road completely free of advertising signs, hot-dog stands, used-car lots and even telephone and power lines.

The hilltop-to-hilltop communications problem was solved long before the invention of the telephone. For ages, gossip and messages have been transmitted by Gomera's "whistling language"—a real language of regulated tones and rhythms representing words, whistled with or without fingers in the mouth, at great volume. (Of course, for closer contact the islanders speak Spanish.) Only a minority of the population keeps the unique language called *silbo* (the whistle) alive today; consider yourself lucky if you come upon a translator.

Gomera is most conveniently reached as a side-trip from Tenerife. The most practical route for tourists is via a modern speedboat ferry which makes the trip between Los Cristianos (Tenerife) and San Sebastián (Gomera) in 40 minutes. Slower ferries, carrying cargo and buses, cars and tractors, take about 75 minutes in either direction.

From the sea Gomera looks bleak and uninspiring, just a colourless mound shrugging stooped shoulders. And, as the ferry approaches, the first sight of the capital, **San Sebastián** (pop. 7,000), is scarcely inspiring. An 11-storey "skyscraper" stands out like a sore thumb in an otherwise sleepy tropical scene.

But the island is far from drab, and the city wears its historic mantle with dignity, for this, after all, is a place never to be forgotten in the annals of human achievement: Columbus took leave of the known world on September 6, 1492, on the voyage which revealed America, from the port of San Sebastián.

One of the local buildings linked with Columbus is the **Church of Our Lady of the Assumption** *(Nuestra Señora de la Asunción),* with its red-tiled roof and sagging wooden doors. A plaque states that Columbus prayed here before sailing westwards. Another tourist attraction is the **Torre del Conde** by the waterfront, now surrounded by a modest banana plantation. Begun in 1440, this was part of a military complex which eventually served to guard the treasures **63**

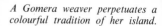

being shipped back from the Indies.

First resident of the tower was the Count of Gomera, Hernán Peraza. His wife, the Spanish beauty Beatriz de Bobadilla, attracted notoriety after the Count had been murdered as he fled from a secret love nest in a Gomera cave. The killers were members of the family of his mistress, a native princess. But Beatriz's truer claim to fame rests on her relationship with Columbus. That the two knew each other is an established fact; how well is a matter of conjecture—and a lot of broad hinting by tour guides on the spot.

Suggestions of a passionate romance are appealing. But nobody really knows what Columbus discovered when he slept here in 1492, 1493 and 1498.

A present-day highlight of San Sebastián is planted on a cliff directly overlooking the harbour. It's a *parador,* a government-run hotel. No expense or effort was spared to make it an outstanding work of architecture and landscaping.

From the capital the main road climbs steeply, a hair-raising drive. You may want to pause for breath in the friendly village of AGULO (pop. 2,000). Adjoining a monumental laurel tree in the village square is the domed Church of San Marco, originally a mosque during a brief period of Moorish occupation in the 17th century. Cliffs riddled with caves tower above the town, and you can hear the hiss of a delicate, slender waterfall.

Steep valleys under intensive cultivation with fruit and

vegetables cheer the scenery much of the way to VALLEHERMOSO, on the island's north side. In this area, but extremely difficult to reach, is a cliff known as **Los Organos.** It consists of thousands of regularly shaped basalt columns rising from the sea like the pipes of some mighty undersea organ. The island's best beaches are also most easily reached by boat.

Fishing is said to be good in Gomera's seas, particularly to the south-west of the island. In the hills, rabbit and other small game abound.

Canaries-style folklore and religious processions bring colour to the Gomera scene. At festivities, there is a distinctive local song and dance, called the Dance of the Drum. No wind or string instruments—only percussion—accompany these ancestral songs, which recount local legends and tales of love.

Gomera handicrafts include some items found nowhere else in the archipelago. Souvenir shops now sell attractive ponchos, doilies, napkins and straw figures. In addition there are unusual, bold ceramics—bowls and jugs created by methods used before the invention of the potter's wheel. On the return trip to Tenerife, distant Mount Teide, aloof and imperious, rises grandly into the sky and seems to dominate the entire Atlantic. It's an unforgettable sight.

Telewhistle: Gomera's own means of crag-to-crag communications. **65**

La Palma

Area: 280 sq. miles
Pop. 80,000

In any competition for the most beautiful island in the world, La Palma, the most north-westerly of the Canaries, would be a worthy contender. It's so enchanting that it's a wonder anyone would want to leave. Yet a high percentage of the island's young men have traditionally emigrated to Latin America, leaving behind some of the most winsome and wistful *señoritas* in all Spain.

La Palma's dimensions are also exceptional. The island's mountain peak, Roque de los Muchachos, rises to 7,950 feet above sea level. That, we are told, makes it the steepest island in the world: no other island has higher mountains within so small an area.

Iberia's F-27 turboprops fly to La Palma from Tenerife in less than half an hour. They land at a modern airport alongside the sea with its terminal built in the traditional Canaries style. The new airport replaces a short airstrip up the mountainside, which had caused earlier travellers some anxious moments.

From the airport it's only a few minutes' drive to the island's port and capital, **Santa Cruz de la Palma.** (Few travellers can avoid initial confusion between names as similar as Santa Cruz de La Palma, Santa Cruz de Tenerife, La Palma, Las Palmas, and other "crosses" and "palms" around the islands.) Entering the outskirts of Santa Cruz de La Palma, the road goes through a 1,500-foot tun-

Santo Domingo de Garafía
Punta Cumplida
Los Sauces
Roque de los Muchachos
2423
Puntagorda
Caldera de Taburiente
Tijarafe
Parque Nacional
Sant. de N.ª Sª de las Nieves
La Cumbrecita
Los Llanos de Aridane
Santa Cruz de la Palma
El Time
Puerto de Tazacorte
El Paso
Aeropuerto
Mazo
San Nicolás
Puerto de Naos
Cueva de Belmaco
N
0   5 km
0   3 miles
Las Caletas
Fuencaliente de la Palma
Punta de Fuencaliente

LA PALMA

nel cut through the wall of an extinct volcanic crater.

The city (population more than 15,000) presents a picture of an appealing metropolis in miniature—clean and bright with traditional and modern architecture side by side. The new offices and blocks of flats blend surprisingly well with the old colonial houses and their wooden balconies painted green, brown or faded red.

Plaza de España, the town's historic centre, is a triangular ensemble a couple of streets inland from the port. On one leg of the triangle is the **Church of the Saviour** *(La Iglesia Matriz de El Salvador),* built in 1503. The ceiling of this big stone church, in the Moorish jigsaw style, is made of *tea,* heart of Canary pine. Next to the church are splendid examples of 18th-century colonial-style mansions. The long leg of the triangle is taken up by the **town hall** *(Ayuntamiento),* built in 1569 during the reign of King Philip II. While the arches of the building's façade are Italian Renaissance, the interior is all Spanish colonial—with formidable carved wooden ceilings, doors, and a ceremonial staircase.

The seafront Avenida de Blas Pérez González is one long array of weather-beaten

Glittering image of patron saint, venerated by La Palma islanders.

balconied houses. The only surprise is the sight of a ship ashore, a full-size replica of Columbus's *Santa María.* The islands have a common proprietary interest in Columbus.

A few miles above the harbour, the **Church of Our Lady of the Snows** *(Nuestra Señora de las Nieves)* contains the richly bejewelled image of the island's patron saint, said to date from the late 14th century. Every August 5, La Palma's festival celebrates Our Lady of the Snows. And every **67**

Santa Cruz de la Palma: Renaissance portal of Church of the Saviour.

five years on this day the image is carried down to the harbour in a colourful pilgrimage procession; the month-long celebrations attract swarms of tourists.

A well engineered but nevertheless difficult road leads through steep, fertile hills, offering superb vistas over the island and the sea. Finally, it climbs into craggy country surrounded by mist-shrouded peaks with green pine trees clinging to the most unlikely ledges. This is **Caldera de Taburiente National Park,** literally inside a volcano. From the vantage point of **La Cumbrecita** you can look down into what is claimed to be the world's largest crater: circumference, about 17 miles; diameter, more than 5½ miles; depth, about 2,300 feet. Fortunately, Taburiente has long been extinct. A peak in the centre is said to have been the sacred altar of the first Guanche natives on the island.

When Spanish forces arrived to conquer La Palma in 1492, all the Guanche princes capitulated but one, Prince Tanausú, who held out with his forces inside the crater in a siege lasting more than seven months. The native leader was finally lured out of his redoubt by a fake offer of peace; the Spaniards then ambushed and captured him. Shipped back to Spain as a trophy of war, the noble Tanausú is said to have died at sea after a hunger strike.

Adventurous hikers with time to spare can organize their own excursions into the crater to explore its many mysteries.

To the west of Taburiente, in a pleasant valley of bananas and palms, almond trees and vineyards, lies the stately colonial town of LOS LLANOS DE ARIDANE (district pop. 12,000). In the Plaza de España, under vast Australian laurel trees, townsfolk sip coffee or a glass of Spanish brandy. A simple white adobe church with a cinderblock belfry faces the traditional town hall with its three

Shades of green, from tropical to nordic, scale La Palma mountain.

arches on the ground floor and carved balconies above.

On the west coast—beyond the enormous ravine called **Barranco de las Angustias** and the mountain **El Time** (pronounced TEE-may)—is the port of TAZACORTE. Good beaches—a rarity on La Palma—and nightlife are the attractions of the area, for nature undoubtedly short-changed the island on the kind of coastline which would draw masses of sunbathers from northern Europe.

The principal road down the south-west side of the island passes through a settlement called SAN NICOLÁS. La Palma's volcanic eruption of 1949 sent an ever-widening stream of molten lava down the green hillside here. You can see it now, petrified and black; the road runs right through the once deadly mass. It takes little imagination to look up the hill and relive those seconds of horror. The lava rushed down towards the sea, where it formed a new little peninsula, now a banana plantation.

The most recent signs of volcanic activity on La Palma can be seen at FUENCALIENTE, a town of 2,000 inhabitants near the southern tip of the island, where the volcano of Tene-

guía erupted in 1971—fortunately with warning and without casualties. For weeks fire and ash spat from the mountain, pouring layer upon layer of lava down to the sea. The local folk are proud of all the publicity they received at the time. Showing their cool nerve, they've set up football goalposts in the ash. You'll appreciate the volcanic soil in quite another light way if you sample the local malmsey *(malvasía)* wine, with its distinctive, rich taste.

The road round the southern part of the island continues in a circuit back to the airport and the capital, Santa Cruz de La Palma. On the way it passes the **cave of Belmaco** *(Cueva de Belmaco)*, which is well worth visiting. It is said to have been a meeting-place of the ancient Guanche tribes, and the large stones with strange circular carved inscriptions are of great interest. Is it prehistoric writing? Is it, as some suggest, the same mysterious language as that of the Easter Islanders or the Incas? Or just meaningless symbols? We may never know. What evidence there may have been was destroyed or looted before the government took official interest in the cave.

El Hierro

Area: 107 sq. miles
Pop. 7,000

Until Columbus, geographers considered El Hierro the end of the world. In some ways, it still looks like that.

From afar it appears little more than a rocky, bleak, windswept island in the middle of the Atlantic Ocean. The harbour of LA ESTACA confirms this impression, consisting as it does of one dreary pier for the mail boat and a couple of creaking inter-island freighters, the harbour-master's office, two bars and a handful of houses climbing a volcanic hillside.

But a closer look at the smallest of the Canaries reveals considerable beauty. The landscape changes suddenly from volcanic to verdant.

A 15-minute taxi ride along a winding uphill road from the harbour or the airport leads to the only Canaries capital located inland. The town of VALVERDE was built high on a mountainside to protect it from recurrent pirate raids. From the belltower-watchtower of its church the sea approaches could be safely surveyed. The sentries also had a view of Tenerife's Mount Teide soaring above the silhouette of the intervening island, Gomera.

For all its pretensions to a population of 5,000, Valverde is really a very small town. In the capital's modern bank, an ink pad is placed on the customers' side of the cashier's cage—a convenience for those who sign their cheques with fingerprints. Valverde is almost totally unprepared for tourism, with only a couple of very basic hotels and restaurants. A government-run tourist hotel has been built on an extremely remote black sand beach far from the town.

Iberia runs a daily 35-minute turboprop flight from Tenerife to El Hierro—the very short landing strip was inaugurated in 1972—but tourist traffic is limited, what with

the lack of tourist facilities and the wild nature of the island. With unexciting swimming conditions and no nightlife, it is strictly for travellers who want to hear the birds sing and see the sun set over the endless sea, the troubled red sky unmarred by power lines or TV aerials.

Among other simple pleasures to be indulged in here are fresh fish, goat's cheese, local white wine and *quesadilla* (pronounced kay-sa-DEEL-ya), a rich cheesecake with a paper-thin crust and a hint of caraway. Travellers leaving El Hierro usually carry boxes of *quesadillas* the way passengers from other places carry their cheap liquor.

From Valverde a reasonably good road follows the backbone of the triangular-shaped island through attractive, undulating countryside. The fields form a jigsaw of stone walls marking the divided ownership of the farms.

The mysterious-looking circular stone fences might well be mistaken for prehistoric shrines or messages to the moon. They are in fact merely practical barriers to protect fig-trees from marauding goats.

The mid-island road climbs to the viewpoint of **Jinama**, with its stirring panoramas of a distant valley rich in banana plantations. The coastline here is called **El Golfo** (the gulf); what we actually see is the inside of an immense volcanic crater, half of which is now beneath the sea.

Alternating with pasture as green as a salad, the island has woodland—including massive pines—and a barren volcanic zone. The texture of the cooled lava takes many forms including some optical illusions to fan any fancy.

At the southern end of the island, reached by a sometimes difficult road, the fishing port of RESTINGA is rich in local colour. A small hotel, unexpectedly perched on the volcanic shore, looks out on to a fascinating blowhole from which a geyser of seawater erupts with every wave.

Every island in the Canaries claims a link with Columbus, but El Hierro is refreshingly modest in this respect. This was, the claim goes, the last land the brave little fleet actually sighted before confronting the unknown. Formalizing Ptolemy and, subsequently, the Arabs, scientists in the early 17th century decided that all maps should begin—or end—at El Hierro; they made it 0° Longitude for the rest of

the world. More than 200 years later the standard meridian was moved to Greenwich. And not many people have heard of El Hierro since then...

Moment of truth, Canaries style: weighing fish on a primitive scale. **73**

What to Do

Sports and Other Activities

With their incomparably mild climate the Canaries make sports a year-round pleasure. Although water sports obviously dominate the scene, there are any number of surprises—from Canaries wrestling to mountain-climbing. In a word, something for everyone—active participant, half-hearted dabbler, or just onlooker.

This is a good place to warn you about the perils of the sun. Unaccustomed as you probably will be to tropical sunshine, a couple of hours of exposure on your first day in the archipelago can burn you a nasty shade of lobster-red. Take it in easy doses until you've secured a base for a real tan. If you're spending long hours out-of-doors, a hat and at least a tee-shirt will make a big difference.

Now, an alphabetical list of sports to choose from:

Boating and sailing

If you arrive in your own yacht, you'll find facilities on all the islands. Six of the seven

principal Canaries have nautical clubs (El Hierro is the exception).

If you've left your yacht at home but would like to hire a boat on the spot, many resorts can come up with sailingboats—or at least *pedalos* (pedal boats). It all depends on local sea conditions.

To experience the real Atlantic Ocean you can sign on for a day-long cruise aboard a schooner or deep-sea fishing motorboat. Excursions are advertised in the major resorts.

Fishing

From the number of islanders who spend their spare time fishing you'll soon deduce that worthwhile results lie in wait. Whether you drop a line off a jetty or wade out into the sea with an elaborate rig, you'll feel yourself in a different league from the anglers at home. Inexpensive tackle is sold in the islands.

If it's really monsters of the deep you're after, take one of the deep-sea-fishing excursions for tourists. One of them advertises "birds, booze, music—and perhaps a shark" for a comparatively small charge. Other outings, with food, water-sports and a full day of sailing are, of course, more expensive.

Of course, if you're a really serious fisherman and would know what to do if a hammerhead shark should bite, then browse around one of the harbours until you find a sea-captain willing to take you out for the day.

Golf

Gran Canaria: Spain's oldest golf club (1891) runs an unusual 18-hole course alongside La Bandama crater, an extinct volcano, 14 kilometres from Las Palmas. A 36-hole course is located near Maspalomas, on the south of the island.

Tenerife: Since 1932 the Golf Club of Tenerife, 18 holes, has operated near Los Rodeos Airport.

Visitors must pay an entrance fee. For the price of visitors' and greens fees, golf lessons and hiring clubs, see page 102 under "Sports".

Horse-riding

At a number of locations in the islands there are ranches where you can hire horses by the hour or day. Refer to page 102 under the entry "Sports" for an idea of the going rates. Instruction is often available.

75

of huffing and puffing. (Beware, though—it's tougher than you think, owing to the rarefied air at that altitude.)

Scuba diving

Equipment may be hired and instruction arranged at various resort centres. Some combination water-sport excursions for tourists include skin-diving lessons.

Surfing

At a few beaches with just the right combination of winds and tides the locals have taken to surfing. It's fairly tame for those with experience in heavier seas, but it's possible to hire a board; instructors are also available.

Hunting and shooting

Quail and rabbit mostly. For details about permits, check with a local or overseas Spanish tourist office or write to the Servicio Nacional de Pesca Fluvial y Caza at Calle Goya, 25, Madrid.

Mountain-climbing

All the islands have mountains enough to explore, but of course *the* summit of all Spain is Tenerife's Mount Teide at 12,198 feet. For the less adventurous, a funicular goes nearly to the summit of Teide, leaving only a few hundred yards

Swimming

Depending on the island, or even which part of the island you're on, conditions can range from black sand to white sand, from rock to hopeless cliffs. Even when you're on the spot, don't trust appearances but ask for advice at your hotel or tourist office. A seemingly calm beach may hide dangerous undercurrents. With few exceptions lifeguards are not available (though first-aid stations are more common). Other facilities vary from nil to the most elaborate seafront bars and changing-room set-ups. In resort centres you can usually hire deck-chairs and umbrellas.

In areas where beaches are too small or dangerous, hotels or municipalities often build salt-water swimming pools. Some of these are enormous and provide an acceptable substitute.

Tennis

Many hotels and apartment complexes have their own courts; some hotels also have tennis teachers on their staff. For the cost of hiring a court or taking a lesson, see page 102 under "Sports".

Water-skiing

At beaches with calm seas and room to spare, water-ski schools have been established. However, water-skiing can turn out to be a rather expensive hobby, particularly if you need private lessons. Average rates are given on page 102 under "Sports"; cheaper ones may be negotiated if you plan a week or two of skiing.

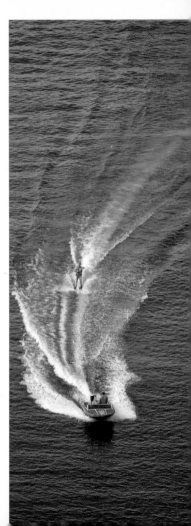

Outdoor sports for varied tastes include fine golf and water-skiing.

Indoor and Spectator Sports

Canaries Wrestling
(lucha canaria)

This sport is a surprising mixture of chivalry and caveman huffing-and-puffing. The barefoot grunt-and-groaners do a great deal of gentlemanly handshaking before, during and after each bout. According to one expert, the roots of Canary wrestling can be traced to ancient Egypt, while others believe the prehistoric Guanches devised it to strengthen muscles, quicken reflexes and amuse the spectators at *fiestas*.

It's a team sport (though only one wrestler from each side competes at a time) with complicated rules and scoring.

But you'll soon appreciate a few of the intricacies, and you may even anticipate the winner before the judges solemnly announce their decision.

Most tourists are introduced to *lucha canaria* at folklore exhibitions. If you'd like to see the real thing, not just a simplified demonstration, go to one of the serious league competitions that are advertised on posters in all the towns.

Cockfights
(peleas de gallos)

Almost every Sunday at midday somewhere in the Canaries you can see cockfights, which are legal and carefully organized. Men make up the majority of the audience, but the presence of women and children indicates that the inherent cruelty makes little impression on the Canarians. The fights are held in an octagonal ring, elevated like a boxing ring. The cocks, well trained and valiant, arrive wrapped in ceremonial red cloths. They are carried out the same way, though the loser

78

is often dead on departure. Lively betting takes place throughout. Each bout lasts about five minutes, to the cheers of the fans and the sympathetic crowing of fighters waiting in the wings.

Basketball. Canarians are great *baloncesto* fans. Every school gymnasium has a busy basketball arena.

Bowling. In major cities and some luxury hotels, full-scale bowling alleys may be found.

Chess. Some of the great masters have played at tournaments in the Canaries; enthusiasm for the game is widespread.

Football. Canaries fans support local soccer teams with noisy gusto. Even the small towns have serious clubs.

Greyhound racing. A greyhound is a *galgo* and a track is called a *canódromo*. Now you know enough to place a bet.

Jai-alai (in Basque country, *pelota*). Said to be the world's fastest ball-game. Pronounced "Hi-Li", it's played in a *frontón,* a sort of giant handball court. Now you *don't* know enough to place a bet.

Vela Latina. Races at sea, a Canaries exclusive—old-fashioned, unsophisticated sailboating against all obstacles. The voluminous sail is known as a "Lateen rig".

Folklore

The folk music of the Canaries is a reminder that the archipelago has always been a bridge between Spain and Spanish America. Some songs sound Spanish, others would be at home in Mexico or Peru. Many can be traced far back into Canaries history. In fact, several centuries ago, Canaries dancing was all the rage in the salons of Europe. The rhythm was catchy, the steps more daring than the customary minuet, and the whole idea rather exotic.

Traditional costumes vary from island to island. On Tenerife, for instance, the girls wear fetching miniature straw hats perched on bright canary-yellow headscarves. Their long skirts have varicoloured vertical stripes. The men wear black felt hats and red vests. The girls of Gran Canaria wear black pillbox hats with pompoms, and flowing skirts with complicated embroidery.

The music, usually played by relatively large groups, includes boleros, fandangos, tangos and other vaguely familiar rhythms. The musicians play guitars and *timples* (small stringed instruments like ukuleles), drums and wooden flutes, and sing.

79

Some songs are known and sung on all the islands, others have local backgrounds. Here is one verse of a song which is popular on Tenerife:

Todas las canarias son como ese Teide gigante: Mucha nieve en el semblante y fuego en el corazón.

Girls of the Canaries are like the great Mount Teide: snowy on the surface but with fire in the heart.

Folklore shows are regular features in all of the tourist centres.

Festivals

What with saints' days as well as universal holidays, one town or another in the islands is almost always celebrating something. Here are a few of the most colourful fiestas.

Lilting rhythms and colourful dress delight tourists at a folklore show.

January

Cabalgata de los Reyes: Processions of the Three Kings: costumes, brass bands, camels in cavalcades. (GRAN CANARIA: Las Palmas/TENERIFE: Santa Cruz, Garachico/GOMERA: Valle Gran Rey.)

February or March

Fiestas del invierno: Winter festivals, Music and colourful parades with comic effigies. (TENERIFE: Puerto de la Cruz, Santa Cruz/LA PALMA: Santa Cruz.) Winter Opera Festival. (GRAN CANARIA: Las Palmas.)

March or April

Semana Santa: Holy Week. Solemn pre-Easter processions in many towns and cities of the archipelago.

Commemoration of the Incorporation of the Islands under the Crown of Castille. (GRAN CANARIA: Las Palmas.)

April or May

Festivales de España: Traditional theatre, ballet, music, arts. (GRAN CANARIA: Las Palmas.)

May

Fiestas de la Cruz: Processions, festivities and fireworks. (EL HIERRO: Valverde, and in all places with "Cruz" (Cross) in their name.

May or June

Fiestas de Corpus Christi: Artistic flower carpets on streets. Processions. (GRAN CANARIA: Las Palmas/TENERIFE: La Orotava, La Laguna/LA PALMA: Villa de Mazo/LANZAROTE: Arucas and Haria.)

June

Romería de San Isidro: Procession of ox-drawn carts with local produce. Colourful costumes. (TENERIFE: La Orotava.)

Fiestas de San Juan: Feast of St. John. Bonfires and other ancient festivities. (TENERIFE: Icod de los Vinos.)

July

Romería de San Benito: Procession of ox-drawn carts. Colourful costumes. (TENERIFE: La Laguna.)

Fiestas del Mar: Festivals of the sea-water sports and religious ceremonies mixed. (TENERIFE: Santa Cruz and Puerto de la Cruz.)

Fiesta de San Buenaventura. (FUERTEVENTURA: Betancuria.)

Romerías de Santiago Apóstol: Festival of St. James: pilgrimage, fireworks. (GRAN CANARIA: Gáldar, San Bartolomé/TENERIFE: Santa Cruz.)

August

Fiesta de Nuestra Señora de la Nieves: Our Lady of the Snows celebrated with religious piety and fun and games. (GRAN CANARIA: Agaete/LA PALMA: Barlovento, Breña Alta and Baja, El Paso, Fuencaliente, Puntallana, San Andrés y Sauces.)

Fiestas de la Asunción: Assumption. Re-enactment of appearance of the Blessed Virgin to Guanche inhabitants of Tenerife. (TENERIFE: Candelaria.)

Fiestas del Cristo del Gran Poder: Local holiday: fireworks, contents and burning of effigy of "idleness" on bonfire. (TENERIFE: Bajamar.)

Fiestas de San Ginés: Concerts, contests, fireworks and parade of camels. (LANZAROTE: Arrecife.)

September

Semana Colón: Christopher Columbus Week. (GOMERA: San Sebastián.)

Romería de la Virgen del Pino: Religious and festive celebrations in honour of Our Lady of the Pine. (GRAN CANARIA: Teror.)

Fiestas del Charco: A festival of traditional Canaries' music, including that of the Guanche people. (GRAN CANARIA: La Aldea near San Nicolás de Tolentino.)

Fiestas del Santísimo Cristo: Floats, flowers and fireworks, processions, sports, classical theatre and poetry readings. (TENERIFE: La Laguna, Tacaronte.)

October

Fiesta de Nuestra Señora de la Luz: Flowers and fireworks. (GRAN CANARIA: Las Palmas.)

Fiesta de Nuestra Señora del Rosario: Religious ceremonies, folklore and sporting events. (FUERTEVENTURA: Puerto del Rosario: GRAN CANARIA: Aguimes, San Bartolomé de Tirajana.)

November

Fiesta del Rancho de Animas: Revival of ancient folklore. (GRAN CANARIA: Teror.)

December

Fiesta de Santa Lucía: The Festival of Lights. (LANZAROTE: Máguez/GRAN CANARIA: Arucas, Gáldar, Santa Lucía.)

The Bullfight

Nothing is more uniquely Spanish—or incomprehensible to the foreigner—than the *fiesta brava,* the bullfight. If you've never experienced this spectacle, you may want to seize the chance in the Canaries. Every winter the bullrings of Gran Canaria and Tenerife schedule *corridas,* often featuring famous *toreros.*

You may not like what you see in the ring, you may swear never to return to it, or you might become an outright *aficionado.* Whatever your reaction, you'll have to admit there's nothing like it in the world: man against bull, a handful of brains against half-a-ton of deadly brawn; and one way or another, death is always the winner.

Understand from the beginning that bullfighting is not intended to be a sport. (Soccer—*fútbol*—is Spain's most popular sport.) A sport is a contest between two equals; in bullfighting the odds are weighted heavily against the bull. The *corrida* is a ritualistic preparation for the bull's death.

The fight is divided into *tercios,* or thirds. The matador meets the fierce bull, takes his measure, and begins to tire him using the big red and yellow *capote.*

Matador sights along his sword as the bull, transfixed, awaits its fate.

In the first *tercio* the *picador,* a mounted spearman, lances the bull's shoulder muscles, and in the second *tercio* the *banderilleros* stab darts into the animal's shoulders.

The matador at this stage returns to taunt the bull with the small, dark red *muleta* or cape, eventually dominating the beast. Finally, as the bull waits for the death he must now sense is inevitable, the matador lunges for the kill.

You may be upset or fascinated or simply confused. But you will have witnessed a violent act which at times contains incredible beauty. With luck you'll come to understand why this ballet of death is considered an art form in Spain.

Flamenco

After the bullfight, flamenco is Spain's best-known entertainment. Moorish in its presumed origins, flamenco bears a striking resemblance to the wailing chants of Arab music. In the Canaries, flamenco shows are popular tourist attractions though there's no guarantee the singers, dancers and guitar players will be up to the best Andalusian standards.

There are two main groups

of flamenco song: one, bouncier and more cheerful, is known as the *cante chico* (a light tune). The second group of songs, called *cante jondo,* deals with love, death, all the human drama, done in the slow, piercing style of the great flamenco singers.

But it's *cante chico* you'll hear at the *tablao flamenco* in the Canaries, the floorshow in nightclub surroundings. Less dramatic and soul-searching, the *cante chico* is basically light-hearted but can be philosophical and touching. It makes for a memorable night out with plenty of excitement and colour.

Vivid sights and sounds of Spanish flamenco have spread to Canaries.

Young visitors to the Canaries find it easy to make friends of all kinds.

For Children

Many hotels have special attractions and trained staff members to amuse children when they're tired of swimming, sunbathing and sandcastles. Beyond this, you have some surprises up your sleeve:

Rent a horse. Stables operating near major resorts supply instruction as well as treks for more advanced riders.

Ride a camel. In Gran Canaria, Tenerife and Lanzarote it's all part of the scene.

Ride a donkey. Gran Canaria's Burro Safari—sightseeing at close quarters.

Tenerife also has its Donkey Safari—a full day's outing.

See a folklore show. Bright costumes and lilting music should delight all children.

Go sailing. Aboard a hired dinghy or excursion schooner.

Go fishing. Bend a hook, bait it with bread, and join the older fishermen down at the seaside.

Look at the flowers. Municipal parks have elaborate gardens, but Tenerife's famous botanical garden (Jardín de Aclimatación) is an unforgettable tropical forest.

Watch the birdie. Tenerife's Loro Park and Gran Canaria's Los Palmitos Park both put on bird shows and exhibit exotic feathered creatures.

Cowboys and Indians. Gran Canaria's Sioux City is a film set come to life: Western-style surprises.

Count the flags. A launch tour of Las Palmas harbour—one of the busiest ports in Spain—reveals ships flying flags of many nationalities.

Follow Columbus. Museums, monuments and mementoes of the great explorer are found throughout the archipelago. They'll help you re-live his adventure.

Cultural Activities

Museums

Canaries museums are very cheap and some do not even charge an entrance fee. Most museums are open until 1 p.m., and reopen at 3 or 4 p.m. until 6 or 7 p.m. (on Saturday mornings only; some close on Sundays).

Lanzarote

Archaeological Museum, San Gabriel Fortress, Arrecife. Small exhibition of prehistoric relics from Lanzarote and the other Canary islands.

Gran Canaria

Casa Colón (Columbus's House), Calle Colón, Vegueta, Las Palmas. This was the governor's mansion, where Columbus stayed in 1492 and on other voyages. Charming architecture; displays of 15th-century maps, weapons, furniture; scale models of his three ships under glass.

Canaries Museum, Calle Dr. Chil, 25, Vegueta, Las Palmas. Fine collection of prehistoric Guanche relics—clothing, jewellery, utensils. Also two large rooms full of skulls and bones—more than 2,000 prehistoric skulls, 11-high in glass cases, like something out of a horror film. Be prepared!

Néstor Museum, Pueblo Canario, Las Palmas. There you'll see the works of Néstor de la Torre, famed artist and designer (1887–1938). Every aspect of Néstor's career is represented, from costume designs and architectural plans to paintings. The artist worked in a style that ranged from turn-of-the-century Art Nouveau to Surrealism and the erotic.

Provincial Fine Arts Museum, Plaza Pilar Nuevo, Las Palmas. Collection of paintings and sculptures by Canarian artists from 18th to 20th centuries.

Tenerife

Archaeological Museum, 2nd floor, Palacio Insular, Calle Bravo Murillo, Santa Cruz de Tenerife. Anthropology collection includes more than a thousand prehistoric skulls. Exhibits of Guanche culture include mummies, pottery, rock engravings and other archaeological finds. See also the hand-operated mill of stone and wood, still in use up to recently on Gomera.

Municipal Museum, Plaza del Príncipe, Santa Cruz de Tenerife. Open weekdays, 3 to 8 p.m., holidays 10 to 1 p.m. Paintings and works of art, primarily by Tenerife artists.

Concerts, Opera, Ballet

Each provincial capital has its own 19th-century opera house where major and minor musical events take place.

In Santa Cruz de Tenerife, the Teatro Guimerá, over 125 years old, with its air of somewhat faded grandeur, is strong on opera. It's also home to the Tenerife Symphony Orchestra, whose season runs from September to May or June.

In Las Palmas, Gran Canaria, the Teatro Pérez Galdós is larger and unexpectedly brighter, with decorations by Néstor de la Torre (see page 43). Opera, *zarzuela* (Spanish musical comedy), ballet and symphony concerts are sometimes advertised without saying where—because everyone knows it's at the Pérez Galdós.

Films

Almost all the films shown commercially in the Canaries have been dubbed into Spanish. Unless you can understand the Spanish dialogue —or read lips in the original language—you're probably out of luck. The price of tickets (see p. 102 under "Entertainment") depends on the location and the film's fame.

Shopping

By royal decree in 1852, the Canary Islands became a duty-free zone, the idea being to encourage the development of the archipelago and its ports as an Atlantic staging base. The plan worked, for the islands now boast the largest, busiest seaports in the whole of Spain. In recent years, however, the duty-free zone has been transformed into a free-trade zone, in which goods are imported without restrictions from all over the world. Luxury tax is still lower than in most countries, and bargains abound.

All the world's drinks are sold at reasonable prices in the islands.

Souk-style market in Puerto de la Cruz has bargains, colour, noise.

Shops are full of good buys—cameras, tape recorders, calculators, watches, perfume, jewellery, leather goods, liquor and tobacco—at prices more advantageous than at any airport shop in the world.

Shopping Hours

Most stores in the Canaries maintain Spanish-style opening hours. They open around 9 a.m. and close for lunch and

siesta at 1 p.m. They reopen at 4 or 5 p.m. and close for the day at 7 or 8 p.m. In the busier tourist resorts a few shops stay open later into the evening, especially at the height of the season.

Best Buys

Depending on the prices you're used to at home, the biggest bargains will probably be imported luxury items (rather than Canary Islands products or even Spanish goods from the mainland). A simple rule of thumb: best buys in the Canaries are items carrying a higher luxury tax in your country. In addition to the bargains in electronics (mostly from Japan), have a look at uncut gems and silver jewellery. Silks and leatherware can prove notable bargains. Some keen shoppers have found good, cheap boutique clothing. Finally, if it isn't too warm to think about furs, check the prices of the elegant mink, sable and fox coats on sale in the fashionable resorts.

Island Products

If you think it's slightly absurd to be buying Hong Kong radios and Thai silk out in the

Atlantic Ocean, consider authentic Canaries handicrafts. They come in many varieties and a wide price range. Perhaps the most celebrated field of local endeavour is embroidery. If you take any tourist excursion you'll probably be shown a handicraft "school" where local girls are engaged in extremely delicate needle work on bedspreads, tablecloths, hand-towels and napkins.

A note of warning: cheap foreign imitations have turned up in the Canaries. Even the experts find it difficult to expose this fraudulent embroidery without minute examination of the stitches. For the non-expert tourist nothing can be done except to try to gauge the reputability of the place where you buy.

Other island items you'll see on sale are ceramics—including charmingly primitive pots from Gomera—and both serious and witty carvings.

By way of inexpensive items from the Canaries, you may be interested in local cigars (including jumbo-sized novelty models) and locally distilled liqueurs with banana, coffee and other tropical flavours. Not the usual tourist ration, but they do carry built-in memories of your holiday.

Spanish Souvenirs

If you're interested in "traditional" souvenirs of the Spanish mainland, you'll find no shortage of Don Quixote statuettes, mock bullfighter swords, inlaid Moorish-style chess sets, imitation antique pistols and bullfight posters (on which your own name can be printed within minutes as star matador).

Where to Shop

It's always wise to compare prices among several shops before you take the plunge. This is particularly so in the Canaries, where almost all prices will look like big bargains when you first arrive. Only when you've become accustomed to the low-duty climate will you be able to discern which bargains are best. In general, prices in the bigger towns are lower than in exclusively tourist developments.

You may be surprised to find that a very high percentage of the shops selling luxury goods in the Canaries are owned by entrepreneurs from India. In most of these "bazaars" prices are flexible; haggling is an accepted part of the shopping process. In any shop where prices are not marked, you may assume that the matter is negotiable.

Non-bargains

As residents of the islands won't hesitate to tell you, the price situation isn't all dreamland. Luxury goods may be giveaways, but the necessities of life are another story. You'll discover this most quickly if you shop in a supermarket. Most food has to be imported, so prices are high—at least in comparison with mainland Spain. The same is true of everyday household goods, clothing and furniture.

Buyer Beware

Rebajas (sales) are often announced in shop windows. Be at your most vigilant. Sometimes the prices have been marked up expressly to be marked down again. Or the merchandise could be imperfect, price-slashed for clearance. The most likely time for a legitimate sale is at the beginning or end of the season, when old goods must be sold to make room for new. If it's a legitimate bargain sale you'll probably see throngs of locals on the scene.

Don't be fooled by urgent-looking signs promising "duty-free" bargains. No shop in the Canaries sells duty-free goods. Duty-free imports ceased years ago.

Last-day Special

When you're about to leave the islands at the end of your holiday, think about buying flowers. Your friends back home have probably never seen real, live *strelitzias*—Bird of Paradise flowers. They're strong, long-lived and portable.

Nightlife

In the principal tourist centres of the Canaries you can find almost anything you may be looking for, from extravagant and formal nightlife to lowdown and rowdy.

World-famous resorts—such as Las Palmas and Maspalomas on Gran Canaria and Puerto de la Cruz on Tenerife—offer lavish possibilities for nightlife. You won't have time to investigate more than a small fraction of the attractions. For a foretaste you might want to book a seat on one of the night excursions run by the travel agencies. They will take you by bus to two or three of the top night-spots; the price includes an introductory drink in each, plus a festive dinner. You may see floor shows of extremely contrasting styles—perhaps wild flamenco, followed by Paris-style chorus girls, and finally demure Canaries folklore. It's all quite respectable and particularly handy for unaccompanied travellers. And no holiday is complete without a visit to the luxury casinos of Gran Canaria and Tenerife.

Elsewhere in the big centres you'll have no trouble finding excitement after dark. There are deafening discos and brassy dance clubs, jazz spots and beer halls. Some spots advertise with neon signs, some by word of mouth, and a few hire touts to lurk in doorways offering instant joy. Most visitors, after a night or two of reconnaissance, seem to settle on one particular place where they feel comfortably at ease—because the music is right, or the prices reasonable, or the clientèle friendly, or the staff *simpático*.

If you're at a more isolated resort, of course, the variety of attractions will be limited. But even in brand-new tourist developments, as soon as the first hotels open their doors, satellite bars and amusement places mushroom. Any time you want a change of pace you can go on one of the organized evening barbecue excursions and enjoy grilled meat, unlimited *sangría* or wine, folklore or flamenco music, dancing and well-planned fun and games.

On almost any afternoon you can enjoy an inspiring start to your nightlife at one of the outdoor cafés, where the price of your apéritif may include the greatest show of all—watching the blazing Atlantic sunset.

Spanish troubadour in medieval garb adds festive tone to party. **91**

Wining and Dining

For gourmets, or ordinary travellers with a taste for adventure, eating and drinking in the Canaries is an immensely satisfying experience. Cosmopolitan cuisine as elaborate as you please exists side by side with local specialities. Whether you choose to be served by tuxedoed waiters in candle-lit continental luxury or by an unshaven but friendly owner in a corner bistro, you'll enjoy eating out in the islands.

Of course, if you're on an all-inclusive package tour with full board you'll be sticking

pretty close to your hotel dining room. This will be filling but boring—a bland international compromise in cooking that neither offends nor particularly pleases. Save a few pesetas for one or two meals away from "home". You'll be amazed at the difference.

Restaurants

Throughout Spain, including the Canaries, restaurants are officially graded by "forks". One fork is the lowest grade, five forks the élite. But ratings are awarded according to the facilities available, not the quality of the food. Many forks on the door guarantee high prices but not necessarily much else. In fact some of the best restaurants in the Canaries have fewer than five forks because their owners prefer it that way, concentrating all efforts on food and wine and disregarding official criteria on the size of the tables or the number of barmen.

One way of choosing a restaurant, aside from studying the menu displayed in the window, is to check how many locals and deeply-tanned expatriates are eating there. If a lot of these value-conscious customers congregate, the chances are you'll get a satisfying meal regardless of the official rating.

Spanish restaurants often offer a *menú del día** (day's special). This is normally three courses including wine at a set price. If a waiter arrives at your table and says, *"¿Menú?"*, he means "Do you wish to order the meal of the day?" If, on the contrary, you want to *read* the menu and choose what to eat, ask for *"La carta, por favor"*.

In almost all restaurants the prices on the menu include taxes and a service charge. But it's customary to leave a tip if you were served satisfactorily. Five per cent is acceptable; 10 per cent is generous.

On the Spanish mainland, late dining hours perplex visitors. Lunch never seems to start until tea-time, and dinner may wait till 10 p.m. However, in the Canaries the tourists have set their own timetable. You can be served a meal at just about any time of day or night. The peak hours are after 1 p.m. for lunch and after 8 p.m. for dinner.

Bars and Cafés

From sunrise to the middle of the night—from the first coffee to the last brandy—the café is a very special institution. Life in Spain could hardly function without it. Breakfast and snacks, coffee and drinks, sweets and sympathy may all be found under one roof—or more likely under the sky, in the Canaries. This is where the mainstream of tourists and local society converge: the Canaries businessmen discuss football over a glass of wine, the tourists dawdle over a beer, watching the new arrivals. A small cup of coffee buys you a ringside seat for as long as you care to stretch it; no one will rush you to leave.

Wines and spirits are served at all hours everywhere in Spain, so don't raise an eyebrow when you see a workman knocking back a shot of colourless liquid fire first thing in the morning. You may also have to get accustomed to the sight of children and dogs in bars. Spaniards consider this perfectly natural, even very late at night (they know the kids have had a long siesta).

Bar and café bills include a service charge, but additional small tips are the custom. Prices are 10 to 15 per cent **93**

---

* For a comprehensive menu reader, ask your bookshop for the Berlitz Spanish–English/English–Spanish pocket dictionary or the new Berlitz EUROPEAN MENU READER.

lower if you stand or sit at the bar instead of being served at a table. Note that *cafeterías* aren't self-service restaurants but glorified snack-bars. The word originally meant a café but service has been expanded to include meals at substantial prices.

Tapas

A *tapa* is a baby-sized portion of food which encourages you to keep drinking instead of going off to dinner. The word *tapa* means "lid" and comes from the old custom of giving a bite of food with a drink, the food served on a saucer atop the glass like a lid. Nowadays, they almost never give away *tapas,* but bars which *sell* them are more popular than ever.

Some specialist bars have a whole counter full of hot and cold appetizers, a Spanish version of smorgasbord. The sort of snacks you're likely to see are shrimp with garlic and parsley; marinated olives; potato salad; baby eels; kidney beans in a vinegar sauce; pickled cauliflower; pigs' trotters in garlic sauce or slices of potato omelet. Just point to what you like.

Vocabulary: *una tapa* is two meatballs at best; *una ración* is half a plateful, and *una porción* of meatballs is a meal. But keep your enthusiasm in check. It's quite possible to spend more for a feast of *tapas* than for a good, conventional dinner.

Breakfast

For Spaniards this is the least significant meal of the day. A large *café con leche* (white coffee) and a piece of bread or pastry is about the size of it. You may want to try distinctive Spanish fritters, *churros,* batter deep fried in oil before your eyes. According to local taste, they are sugared and dunked in coffee or hot chocolate before being eaten.

In deference to foreign habits, most hotels and some cafés nowadays offer a *desayuno completo* of orange juice, toast and coffee, perhaps with bacon and eggs.

If Canaries coffee is too strong for your taste you can ask for hot water and a sachet of instant coffee in many cafés.

Canaries Cuisine

Don't underrate the local cooking. It might not win any gourmet prizes but it's wholesome, filling and often delicious. Unfortunately, it's

Seafood fresh from the Atlantic is fundamental to Canaries cuisine.

easier to find a "genuine Swedish smörgåsbord" or pizzeria than a native Canaries restaurant. When you find the real thing, look for these items on the menu or blackboard:

Rancho canario—a rich vegetable soup thickened with *gofio,* the Canaries staff of life. *Gofio* was first eaten by the prehistoric Guanches. It was made of crushed barley or rye. Now it's usually wholemeal or maizemeal, toasted and milled.

Garbanzo compuesto— chick-pea stew with potatoes, also with the added *gofio* flavour.

Papas viudas (literally, widow potatoes)—roast potatoes with carrots, peas, parsley, olives, green pepper, ham, onion.

Sancocho—a stew of salted sea-bass with white potatoes, sweet potatoes, assorted cooked vegetables, and a piquant sauce called *mojo picón.*

Papas arrugadas (literally, wrinkled potatoes)—potatoes baked in salt, eaten skin and all, with *mojo picón*, the spicy sauce which comes in green or red varieties. The sauce normally contains hot peppers, oil, garlic and saffron. Try it very tentatively before you pour it on.

Fish: Surrounded by the Atlantic Ocean, the Canarians naturally consider fish a vital part of their diet. You'll find nearly any kind of seafood you could wish for, from octopus to swordfish, mostly grilled. Some distinctive Canaries fish varieties are *vieja, cabrilla* and *cherne.*

Cheeses: Goat's cheeses, varying from island to island and year to year, are worth sampling. Some of the locals, seeing a big round cheese in the market, can press it with a thumb and tell you where it comes from and whether it will be superlative or just satisfactory.

Sweets: Cakes and pastries in many original styles may be found throughout the archipelago. El Hierro is notable for its *quesadilla,* a miniature cheesecake. Elsewhere look for Canarian nougat, made with *gofio* and honey, and *bombón gigante* (giant sweet), a nutty chocolate mousse.

Spanish Cuisine

Since the Canaries are a part of Spain, and since tourists from the peninsula do make up a fair percentage of the visitors, good Spanish restaurants may be found in the islands. Look for these mainland specialities:

Sopa de ajo, a thick soup of finely chopped garlic, with paprika, breadcrumbs, eggs.

Huevos a la flamenca. Baked eggs, asparagus, red pepper and peas atop a sausage-and-ham base.

Tortilla española, Spanish potato omelet.

Fabada asturiana, a hearty stew of beans, ham, pork, sausage, onions, garlic, saffron, etc.

Paella—pronounced pye-AIL-ya—named after the large black iron pan in which it's cooked. Ingredients: saffron rice, prawns, mussels, shrimp, chicken, rabbit, sausage, peas, red peppers, etc.

Wines and Spirits

In Elizabethan times, Canaries wine was served at all the top tables of Europe. Tastes have become more sophisticated, but you'll still enjoy trying the local wines. Incidentally, they are normally more expensive than table wines imported from the mainland.

Several of the wines originate from volcanic soil and have a distinctively earthy flavour. The most historic types of Canaries wine are malmsey *(malvasía)* and muscatel. These tend to be sweet but there are drier varieties with distinctive bouquets. Elsewhere you'll find local clarets and, more rarely, rosés. You're more likely to be offered Canaries wine in country restaurants and wine shops than in the cities. In such places the "house" wine may be served unaffectedly in a used mineral water bottle. Don't let this put you off. On the contrary, it simply means the neighbourhood wine is drawn straight from the cask.

Rum, a sugar-based liquor, may conjure up visions of the Caribbean, but it's also made in the Canaries and is extremely popular with the locals. It's often drunk mixed with cola in a *Cuba libre*.

Local distilleries also produce liqueurs with fruit bases—banana particularly, but also coffee, orange, and other tropical flavours.

Sangría is a popular tourist drink throughout Spain. It's a mixture of red wine, orange and lemon juice, brandy, mineral water, slices of fruit and plenty of ice. A refreshing warm-weather punch, but you may find it too strong and heavy to drink with lunch.

Sherry *(Jerez),* Spain's most famous wine, is fortified with brandy. There are three main types—*fino* (pale and dry), *amontillado* (darker and stronger) and *oloroso* (dark and sweet).

Spanish brandy, called colloquially *coñac*, is said to have a less delicate taste than French cognac. The modest prices of the Canaries enable you to compare them at length.

The same goes for all the world's notable alcoholic beverages, on sale in astounding variety at eye-popping prices in just about every supermarket. Whether you want to experiment with Venezuelan lager, Finnish vodka or American bourbon, you'll find what you're looking for—plus much, much more.

To Help You Order...

Do you have a set menu?   **¿Tiene un menú del día?**

I'd like a/an/some...   **Quisiera...**

milk	**leche**	mineral water	**agua mineral**
beer	**una cerveza**	potatoes	**patatas, papas**
bread	**pan**	salad	**una ensalada**
coffee	**un café**	sandwich	**un bocadillo**
dessert	**un postre**	soup	**una sopa**
fish	**pescado**	sugar	**azúcar**
fruit	**fruta**	tea	**un té**
ice-cream	**un helado**	(iced) water	**agua (fresca)**
menu	**la carta**	wine	**vino**

...and Read the Menu

aceitunas	olives
ajo	garlic
albaricoques	apricots
albóndigas	meatballs
almejas	baby clams
anchoas	anchovies
anguila	eel
arroz	rice
asado	roast
atún	tunny (tuna)
bacalao	codfish
besugo	sea bream
bistec	beef steak
boquerones	fresh anchovies
caballa	mackerel
calamares	squid
(a la romana)	(deep fried)
callos	tripe
cangrejo	crab
caracoles	snails
cebollas	onions
cerdo	pork
champiñones	mushrooms
chorizo	a spicy pork sausage
chuleta	chops
cordero	lamb
dorada	sea-bass
ensalada	salad
entremeses	hors-d'oeuvre
estofado	stew
filete	fillet
flan	caramel mould
frambuesas	raspberries
fresas	strawberries
frito	fried
galletas	biscuits (cookies)
gambas	shrimp
granadas	pomegranates
guisantes	peas
helado	ice-cream
higos	figs
huevo	eggs
jamón	ham
judías	beans
langosta	spiny lobster
langostino	prawn
lenguado	sole
limón	lemon
lomo	loin
manzana	apple
mariscos	shellfish
mejillones	mussels
melocotón	peach
merluza	hake
naranja	orange
ostras	oysters
pastel	cake
pescado	fish
pescadilla	whiting
pez espada	swordfish
pimiento	green pepper
piña	pineapple
plátano	banana
pollo	chicken
postre	dessert
pulpitos	baby octopus
queso	cheese
salchichón	salami
salmonete	red mullet
salsa	sauce
sandía	watermelon
sopa	soup
ternera	veal
tortilla	omelet
tostada	toast
trucha	trout
uvas	grapes
verduras	vegetables

How to Get There

Considering the wide choice of ways to go and the complexity of fares and regulations, you'd be well advised to put yourself into the hands of a reliable travel agent. It's the best way of meeting your timetable and your budget.

BY AIR

Scheduled Flights

From the British Isles: there are non-stop flights to Tenerife and Las Palmas, plus a variety of one-stop services, mostly via Madrid. Dublin, Edinburgh and Manchester have one-stop services to Tenerife. Similarly there are direct, one-stop services to Las Palmas from Belfast, Glasgow and Manchester.

Providing your holiday arrangements are fairly flexible you could take advantage of the money-saving Excursion fare on scheduled flights. To be eligible you may have to stay on the islands for a specified period.

From North America: there is a non-stop service between New York and Tenerife/Las Palmas. You can also fly via Madrid or Lisbon.

Special tickets, such as APEX (advance purchase excursion fare), permit considerable reductions on most scheduled flights.

Charter Flights and Package Tours

From the UK: British travel agents and the government have worked out special guarantees to protect holiday-makers in case a tour company should go out of business. The package tour—with flight, hotel and meals included—remains a popular way of visiting the Canaries and is usually the cheapest.

Read your contract carefully before you sign. Most tour operators recommend a "cancellation insurance", a modestly priced additional safeguard which means you lose no money if illness or accident forces you to cancel your holiday.

From North America: all-inclusive Canaries holidays, usually by charter jet, now operate from the United States. Accommodation in a hotel or apartment is normally included for little more than the price of a scheduled air ticket alone.

BY SHIP

From the UK: a number of shipping lines operate services to Gran Canaria, Lanzarote and Tenerife from Southampton. Ships from principal continental European ports, such as Marseilles and Genoa, also serve the Canaries.

From North America: passenger and cargo ships make regular crossings from New York. Non-scheduled freighters are difficult because of a strict limit on the number of passengers. For luxury voyages, check on cruise-ship sailings; many stop at Las Palmas or Tenerife, or both.

BY TRAIN AND SHIP

Good though crowded trains link Spain with all parts of Europe. If you're touring by rail you can connect with one of the regular Spanish passenger-and-mail ships from Barcelona or Cádiz to the Canaries.

When to Go

The sunny Canaries are particularly tempting during the grim months of Europe's winter. This is high-season, when prices are at their peak. Hotel rates drop after Easter. remaining low until November.

Despite the popular description of the Canaries' climate as "eternal springtime", it is virtually impossible to generalize about the islands. At any moment it may be pouring with chilly rain on Gomera while sunbathers frolic on Fuerteventura. It's also common for conflicting weather patterns to compete on different sides and different altitudes of the same island: this is particularly applicable to the islands with high mountain ranges, such as Tenerife.

As a rule of thumb, the easterly islands are drier and warmer than the westerly ones. Another pattern: sunnier, warmer weather is likely to be found on the south side of an island. Lanzarote and Fuerteventura are normally about 3 °C warmer than Gran Canaria.

And be prepared for legendary winds: in February, March or April the *alisio*, a cold and humid intruder from the north-west, and in autumn, the famous *sirocco*.

TENERIFE		J	F	M	A	M	J	J	A	S	O	N	D
Air	F	64	62	64	64	68	71	74	75	74	70	69	64
temperature	C	17	16	17	18	21	22	23	24	23	22	20	18
Water	F	68	64	66	68	68	70	72	73	72	72	68	66
temperature	C	20	18	19	20	20	21	22	23	22	22	20	19
Rainy days		7	7	5	3	1	0	0	1	2	6	7	6

GRAN CANARIA		J	F	M	A	M	J	J	A	S	O	N	D
Air	F	62	62	62	64	66	69	72	73	73	71	67	63
temperature	C	17	16	17	17	19	20	22	23	22	22	19	17
Water	F	64	64	64	64	66	68	70	72	72	72	70	66
temperature	C	18	18	18	18	19	20	21	22	22	22	21	19
Rainy days		1	3	3	3	1	0	0	0	0	2	4	5

Figures shown are approximate monthly averages.

Planning Your Budget

To give you an idea of what to expect, here are some average prices in Spanish pesetas. However, they must be regarded as approximate; inflation in Spain, as elsewhere, rises steadily.

Baby-sitters. From 350 ptas. per hour.

Bicycle and motorscooter hire. Bicycles around 150 ptas. per hour, motorscooters 800 ptas. per day, 4,500 ptas. per week, mopeds 500 ptas. per day, 2,000 ptas. per week.

Car hire (international company, Tenerife; all prices with unlimited mileage). *Seat 127* 2,550 ptas. per day, 15,300 ptas. per week. *Seat Ritmo* 3,650 ptas. per day, 21,900 ptas. per week. *Seat 131 Mirafiori* 4,600 ptas. per day, 27,600 ptas. per week. Add 3% tax.

Cigarettes. Spanish brands from 25 ptas., imported from 65 ptas.

Entertainment. Cinema 150 ptas., flamenco nightclub (entry and first drink) 1,000–2,500 ptas.

Hairdressers. *Man's* haircut 400 ptas. *Woman's* haircut 500 ptas., shampoo and set 600–1,000 ptas., blow-dry 700–1,000 ptas.

Hotels (double room with bath in season). ***** 5,000–8,000 ptas., **** 3,000–6,000 ptas., *** 2,600–4,500 ptas., ** 1,500–2,500 ptas., * 600–1,500 ptas.

Meals and drinks. Continental breakfast from 200 ptas., lunch/dinner in fairly good establishment 1,000 ptas., coffee from 55 ptas., Spanish brandy from 90 ptas., beer (local) from 55 ptas., soft drink from 55 ptas. Prices in 4- and 5-star hotels are much higher.

Shopping bag. Bread (500 g.) 55–75 ptas., butter (250 g.) 80–90 ptas., 6 eggs 60 ptas., beefsteak (500 g.) 500 ptas., coffee (250 g.) 170–190 ptas., wine (bottle) from 85 ptas., fruit juice (1 litre) from 97 ptas.

Sports. *Golf* green fee with all membership facilities, October–March 1,500 ptas. per day, April–September 1,000 ptas., hire of clubs 400 ptas. per day, caddy 400 ptas. *Horse riding* 700 ptas. per hour with reduction for half or full day. *Tennis* from 400 ptas. per hour, instruction from 1,000 ptas. per hour. *Water skiing* from 700 ptas. per round, half-hour lesson 2,000 ptas., one hour 3,500 ptas.

Taxi (Tenerife). Meter starts at 55 ptas., but fixed prices for most journeys.

BLUEPRINT for a Perfect Trip

An A-Z Summary of Practical Information and Facts

A star (*) following an entry indicates that relevant prices are to be found on page 102.

Listed after some basic entries is the appropriate Spanish translation, usually in the singular, plus a number of phrases that should help you when seeking assistance.

Contents

A **AIRPORT** *(aeropuerto).* All the islands except Gomera now have airports with modern facilities. Scheduled international flights serve Tenerife and Gran Canaria. Frequent shuttle flights by Iberia jets or turboprops go on to the lesser islands. The archipelago's busiest airport is at Gando, Gran Canaria, about half-way between Las Palmas and the south-coast resorts. Its huge new terminal can handle 10,000 people at a time, but there are no signboards announcing flights so you must listen carefully to the loudspeaker.

Every airport in the archipelago, large or small, is served by taxis, car-hire firms and airline buses. Souvenir shops, bars, porters and other amenities are also found everywhere.

Porter!	¡Mozo!
Taxi!	¡Taxi!
Where's the bus for…?	¿De dónde sale el autobús para…?

B **BABY-SITTERS*** *(señorita para cuidar niños.)* The larger hotels provide this facility as a matter of course. Prices depend on the time of day and the length of the engagement.

Can you get me a baby-sitter for tonight?	¿Puede conseguirme una señorita para cuidar los niños esta noche?

BICYCLE and MOTORSCOOTER HIRE* *(bicicletas; scooters de alquiler).* A practical, enjoyable way to go exploring is to hire two-wheeled transport able to get you over the most narrow, bumpy paths. In a few resorts, bicycles—even tandem models—may be hired by the hour or day. Rates vary enormously.

Vespas, squat motorscooters of up to 175 cc., powerful enough to transport driver and passenger with ease, can be hired by the day or by the week.

Mobylettes are more elementary 49 cc. mopeds (motorbikes) requiring little mechanical knowledge; passengers not recommended. Maximum speed is about 30 kilometres per hour (20 miles per hour).

Remember that the minimum age for riding a motorcycle or moped under 75 cc. is 16; for vehicles over 75 cc., 18 (plus driving licence); and that the wearing of crash helmets is obligatory, whatever the capacity of the engine.

I'd like to hire a bicycle.	Quisiera alquilar una bicicleta.
What's the charge per day/week?	¿Cuánto cobran por día/semana?

CAMPING *(camping)*. Officially approved camping sites are extremely rare in the Canaries. According to the latest report only one operates on Gran Canaria. If all else fails, there is no shortage of caves in the islands. Some haven't been lived in for hundreds of years.

May we camp here?	**¿Podemos acampar aquí?**

CAR HIRE* *(coches de alquiler)*. See also DRIVING. Car hire firms in the Canaries handle an unusually wide variety of cars, from the humble Seat 127 to sumptuous Chryslers and Mercedes. The rates vary accordingly. Because these are islands, unlimited mileage is usually free. But this is by no means universal; check your contract carefully. The rates given on page 102 are sample prices of major operators. Local firms often charge less.

A deposit, as well as an advance payment of the estimated rental charge, is generally required, although holders of major credit cards are normally exempt from this. A tax is added to the total bill. Third-party insurance is automatically included.

Normally you must be over 21 and hold an international driving licence. In practice, British, American and European licences are accepted in almost all situations.

I'd like to hire a car (tomorrow).	**Quisiera alquilar un coche (para mañana).**
for one day/a week	**por un día/una semana**
Please include full insurance.	**Haga el favor de incluir el seguro todo riesgo.**

CIGARETTES, CIGARS, TOBACCO* *(cigarrillos, puros, tabaco)*. Comparatively low duties make cigarettes one of the most obvious bargains, and bought by the carton in supermarkets they're even cheaper. Imported foreign brands are up to three times the price of local makes. Most Spanish cigarettes are made of strong, black tobacco with a high nicotine content.

Canary-made cigars are highly regarded by connoisseurs. Pipe smokers find the local tobacco somewhat rough, but imported brands are widely available.

A packet of.../A box of matches, please.	**Un paquete de.../Una caja de cerillas, por favor.**
filter-tipped	**con filtro**
without filter	**sin filtro**

C **CLOTHING.** Though summer and beach wear are obviously on your mind, don't forget sweaters or wraps for evenings. For excursions to higher altitudes, warm clothing and sturdy shoes should be packed. During the winter a raincoat may well come in handy. In spite of the casual atmosphere in most resorts, clients of luxury hotels and restaurants tend to dress formally in the evening, dinner jacket and all.

In Spain, where wearing a bikini was once considered daring, topless bathing has become fairly common. Though officially a misdemeanour, the authorities usually turn the other way—if it's done discreetly.

When you're walking to or from the beach, shirts or informal dresses should be worn over bathing costumes; the same goes for in town. More sober clothing—no Bermuda shorts or very short skirts—should, of course, be worn when visiting churches.

COMMUNICATIONS

Post offices are for mail and telegrams; normally you cannot make telephone calls from them.

Hours vary slightly from town to town, but routine postal business is generally transacted:
from 9 a.m. to 2 p.m., Monday to Friday; 9. a.m. to 1 p.m. on Saturday.

Post offices usually keep certain windows open longer for **telegraph** and some other services. So don't be angry if an official won't sell you stamps after 2 p.m.

You can avoid the crowds and buy your postage stamps (*sello* or *timbre*) at any tobacconist's *(tabacos)*.

Postboxes are painted silver, striped in the national colours—red, yellow and red. If one of the slots is marked *extranjero*, it's for foreign-destination mail.

Poste restante (general delivery): If you don't know ahead of time where you'll be staying, you can have your mail addressed poste restante *(lista de correos)* at whichever town is most convenient:

> Mr. John Smith
> Lista de Correos
> Puerto de la Cruz
> Tenerife, Spain

Take your passport to the post office as identification.

Telephone *(teléfono):* For local calls, street-corner phone booths or public telephones in bars and restaurants require a stock of 5-, 25- or 50-peseta coins inserted before dialling. Then you keep dropping in coins as they're swallowed.

For overseas calls, consult your hotel switchboard operator or go to the telephone office in the nearest town. To reverse the charges, ask for *cobro revertido.* For a personal (person-to-person) call, specify *persona a persona.*

Telephone Spelling Code

A	Antonio	**G**	Gerona	**M**	Madrid	**S**	Sábado
B	Barcelona	**H**	Historia	**N**	Navarra	**T**	Tarragona
C	Carmen	**I**	Inés	**Ñ**	Ñoño	**U**	Ulises
CH	Chocolate	**J**	José	**O**	Oviedo	**V**	Valencia
D	Dolores	**K**	Kilo	**P**	París	**W**	Washington
E	Enrique	**L**	Lorenzo	**Q**	Querido	**X**	Xiquena
F	Francia	**LL**	Llobregat	**R**	Ramón	**Y**	Yegua
						Z	Zaragoza

Where is the (nearest) post office?	**¿Dónde está la oficina de correos (más cercana)?**
Have you received any mail for…?	**¿Ha recibido correo para…?**
A stamp for this letter/ postcard, please.	**Por favor, un sello para esta carta/tarjeta.**
express (special delivery)	**urgente**
airmail	**vía aérea**
registered	**certificado**
I want to send a telegram to…	**Quisiera mandar un telegrama a…**
Can you get me this number in…	**¿Puede comunicarme con este número en…?**

COMPLAINTS. By law, all hotels and restaurants must have official complaint forms *(hoja de reclamaciones)* and produce them on demand. The original of this triplicate document should be sent to the regional office of the Ministry of Tourism, one copy remains with the establishment complained against and you keep the third sheet. Merely asking for a complaint form is usually enough to resolve most matters since tourism authorities take a serious view of complaints and your host wants to keep both his reputation and his licence.

C In the rare event of major obstruction, when it is not possible to call in the police, write directly to the Subsecretario del Turismo, Sección de Inspección y Reclamaciones:

Alcalá, 44, Madrid.

If your problem is bad merchandise or car repairs, remember that in Spain consumer protection is in its early days. Seek out the owner or manager if you really think you've been wronged. Failing that, the local tourist office may help. In outrageous cases go to the police. Even if they cannot help, they'll be able to take action if they receive several complaints against any one firm.

CONSULATES *(consulado)*

Santa Cruz de Tenerife:
British Consulate*: Calle de Suárez Guerra, 40; tel. 24 20 00

Las Palmas de Gran Canaria:
British Consulate*: Calle Alfredo L. Jones, 33; tel. 26 25 08
U.S. Consulate: General Primo de Rivera, 5; tel. 27 12 59

Almost all Western European countries have consular offices in Santa Cruz and/or Las Palmas.
   If you run into trouble with the authorities or the police, consult your consulate for advice.

Where's the British/American consulate?	**¿Dónde está el consulado británico/americano?**
It's very urgent.	**Es muy urgente.**

CONVERTER CHARTS. For fluid and distance measures, see page 111. Spain uses the metric system.

Temperature

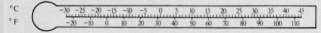

Weight

* Also for citizens of Commonwealth countries.

Length

COURTESIES. See also MEETING PEOPLE. Canarians tend to be easygoing people and share with their mainland cousins a belief in the virtues of *mañana:* don't try to rush them. Far from helping, it might lengthen the delay. Smile and take your time, too.

In a restaurant you must ask for your bill *("la cuenta, por favor").* No waiter will offer it spontaneously, even if you sit for an hour, lest it seem he were pushing you out into the street.

Other courtesies that matter: a simple *"buenos días"*—"good morning" or "good day"—will go a long way. It should precede *any* conversation, even if you stop somebody in the street to ask directions or walk into a bar to order a drink.

Taking pictures in the Canaries is a delight, but if a quaintly dressed country woman turns her back on your camera, don't pester her. You'll see plenty of photogenic models in even more colourful costumes at the folklore show.

If you're driving, you're expected to extend every courtesy to smaller or less powerful vehicles on the road. Canarians are most unimpressed by big, powerful cars. They are also extremely sensitive to any show of superiority.

Visitors to Spain sometimes feel embarrassed at being stared at in out-of-the-way villages. In the Canaries, staring isn't considered rude. Simply stare right back, and say *"buenos días"*, and you've probably made a friend.

How do you do?	**Encantado de conocerle** (**conocerla** when addressing a woman).
How are you?	**¿Cómo está usted?**
Very well, thank you.	**Muy bien, gracias.**

CRIME and THEFT *(crimen; robo).* Hotels recommend that you use their safe for all valuables, including your passport. (Passports are said to fetch $1,000 on the black market.) Beware of pickpockets, particularly in crowded places such as markets and buses.

I want to report a theft.	**Quiero denunciar un robo.**

D **DRIVING IN THE CANARIES**

Arrival: Unless you plan to stay for a long time, it's unlikely that you'd want to ship your car all the way to the Canaries. But if you do, this is what you'll need:

International Driving Licence	Car registration papers	Green Card (an extension to your regular insurance policy, making it valid for foreign countries)
	Nationality plate or sticker	

Recommended: a Spanish bail bond. If you injure somebody in an accident in Spain, you can be detained while the accident is being investigated. This bond will bail you out. Apply to your insurance company.

The nationality sticker must be prominently displayed on the back of your car. If your car has seat belts, it's obligatory to use them; fines for non-compliance are up to 5,000 pesetas per person. A red reflecting warning triangle is compulsory when driving on motorways (expressways). Motorcycle riders and their passengers must wear crash helmets.

Driving conditions: The rules are the same as in mainland Spain and the rest of the Continent: drive on the right, overtake on the left, yield right of way to all vehicles coming from your right.

Depending on the island and the district, roads vary strikingly from six-lane motorways (expressways) to primitive tracks. Many roads are narrow and twisting, though actually delightful—provided you're not in a hurry. Remember that quaint local attractions can become deadly perils on the road—horse-drawn carts, donkeys, sheep, goats and old folk who haven't quite adapted to the new age of transport. When passing through villages, drive with extra care to avoid children darting out of doorways and older folk strolling in the middle of the road, particularly after dark. A 60-kilometre-per-hour speed limit in residential areas is strictly enforced.

Parking: Many towns charge a token fee for parking during working hours; the cities more. The attendants are often disabled, and it's usual to round off the price of the ticket upwards.

It is forbidden to park the car facing oncoming traffic.

Traffic police: Armed Civil Guards *(Guardia Civil)* patrol the roads on **110** powerful black motorcycles. These tough-looking *hombres* are courteous and will stop to help anyone in trouble. But they're inflexible with law-breakers.

In towns, the municipal police—sometimes flamboyantly uniformed—handle traffic control.

The most common offences include passing without flashing your lights, travelling too close to the car in front, and driving with a burned-out head- or rear-lamp. (Spanish law requires you to carry a set of spare bulbs at all times.)

Fluid measures

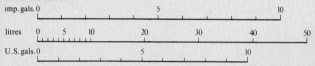

Distance

Breakdowns: Because of the heavy workload, repairs may take longer than they would at home. Spare parts are readily available for all major makes of cars, regardless of nationality.

Road signs: Most road signs are the standard pictographs used throughout Europe. However, you may encounter these written signs in the Canaries:

Aparcamiento	Parking
Atención	Caution
Blandones	Soft verge (shoulders)
Ceda el paso	Give way (Yield)
Despacio	Slow
Desprendimientos	Landslides
Desviación	Diversion (Detour)
Escuela	School
Estacionamiento prohibido	No parking
Obras	Road works
¡Pare!	Stop
Peatones	Pedestrians
Peligro	Danger
Salida de camiones	Lorry (Truck) exit

D | (International) Driving Licence | **carné de conducir (internacional)**
| Car registration papers | **permiso de circulación**
| Green Card | **carta verde**

| Can I park here? | **¿Se puede aparcar aquí?**
| Are we on the right road for…? | **¿Es ésta la carretera hacia…?**
| Fill the tank please, top grade. | **Llénelo, por favor, con super.**
| Check the oil/tires/battery. | **Por favor, controle el aceite/los neumáticos/la batería.**

| I've had a breakdown. | **Mi coche se ha estropeado.**
| There's been an accident. | **Ha habido un accidente.**

DRUGS. As elsewhere in Spain, the authorities in the Canaries have no sympathy for narcotics of any sort nor for their users. Prison sentences for drug offences range from 20 months to 20 years. Suspects may have to wait up to 18 months for trial—in jail.

E **ELECTRIC CURRENT** *(corriente eléctrica)*. Both 110- and 220-volt 50-cycle current may be found, usually depending upon the age of the building. To play it safe, ask at your hotel desk.

If you have trouble with an appliance ask your desk clerk or travel agency courier to recommend an *electricista*.

| What's the voltage—110 or 220? | **¿Cuál es el voltaje—ciento diez o doscientos veinte?**

| an adaptor | **un adaptador**
| a battery | **una pila**

EMERGENCIES *(urgencia)*. If your hotel desk clerk isn't handy to help, here are a few emergency telephone numbers:

	Santa Cruz de Tenerife	Las Palmas de Gran Canaria
Municipal police	091	20 23 22
Fire	22 00 80	24 31 00
Hospital	64 24 00	23 41 22

Depending on the nature of the emergency, refer to the separate entries in this section such as CONSULATES, MEDICAL CARE, POLICE, etc.

ENTRY FORMALITIES and CUSTOMS. Most visitors, including citizens of Great Britain, the U.S.A., Canada and Eire, require only a valid passport—no visa, no health certificate—to enter Spain. Visitors from Australia, New Zealand and South Africa, however, must have a visa.

The formalities upon arrival in the Canaries are generally so informal that passports are not even stamped. If you expect to remain longer than 90 days, a Spanish consulate or tourist office can advise you.

Since the Canary Islands are a free-trade zone, there is no restriction on what you may bring with you as a tourist. However, it would be absurd to buy duty-free cigarettes or spirits at your airport of departure. Prices in ordinary stores in the Canaries are much lower than at any airport in the world.

Spanish tourists are severely restricted in what they can carry back to the mainland, but foreigners may take away their heart's desire in cut-rate purchases. The worry comes on arrival home.

The following chart shows what main duty-free items you may take back into your own country:

Into:	Cigarettes	Cigars	Tobacco	Spirits	Wine
Australia	200	or 250 g. or	250 g.	1 l. or	1 l.
Canada	200	and 50 and	900 g.	1.1 l. or	1.1 l.
Eire	200	or 50	or 250 g.	1 l. and	2 l.
N. Zealand	200	or 50	or ½ lb.	1 qt. and	1 qt.
S. Africa	400	and 50 and	250 g.	1 l. and	1 l.
U.K.	200	or 50	or 250 g.	1 l. and	2 l.
U.S.A.	200	and 100 and	*	1 l. or	1 l.

* a reasonable quantity

Currency restrictions: While there's no limit on what a non-resident may import or export in foreign currencies or traveller's cheques, he cannot bring into Spain more than 150,000 pesetas—which must be declared upon arrival—or leave the country with more than 20,000 pesetas.

GUIDES and INTERPRETERS. Local tourist offices can direct you to qualified guides and interpreters and tell you what they charge.

Note that rates are about 30% higher during the evening, Sundays and holidays, and that interpreters are allowed to establish their own fees.

In most centres, an English-speaking guide can be hired at short notice.

We'd like an English-speaking guide.	**Queremos un guía que hable inglés.**
I need an English interpreter.	**Necesito un intérprete de inglés.**

HAGGLING. Any place where prices are clearly marked probably sticks to those prices, and an attempt to haggle might be frowned on. Arab and Indian stores, on the other hand, traditionally engage in bargaining. Try offering half the asked price and see if a compromise can be reached.

H **HAIRDRESSERS*.** Most large hotels have their own salons and the standard is generally very good. Men's barbers are called *barbería*, women's salons, *peluquería*. Prices are far lower in neighbourhood salons in the towns than in the resorts and chic hotels.

The following vocabulary will help:

I'd like a shampoo and set.	**Quiero lavado y marcado.**
I want a...	**Quiero...**
haircut	**un corte de pelo**
razor cut	**un corte a navaja**
blow-dry (brushing)	**un modelado**
permanent wave	**una permanente**
colour rinse/hair-dye	**un champú colorante/un tinte**
manicure	**una manicura**
Don't cut it too short.	**No me lo corte mucho.**
A little more off (here).	**Un poco más (aquí).**

HITCH-HIKING (*auto-stop*). In Spain, hitch-hiking is permitted everywhere. The odds on catching a lift are good in the islands, since cars are so numerous.

Can you give me/us a lift to...?	**¿Puede llevarme/llevarnos a...?**

HOTELS and ACCOMMODATION* (*hotel; alojamiento*). Spanish hotel prices are no longer government-controlled. Prices range from a
few hundred pesetas per night for a simple but always clean double

room in a village *fonda* (inn) to several thousand pesetas for a double in a luxurious five-star hotel. Before the guest takes the room he fills out a form indicating the hotel category, room number and price and signs it. Breakfast is normally included in the room rate.

Off-season (see WHEN TO GO, page 101) rates are theoretically lower, and vacancies, of course, are much more numerous.

An increasingly important aspect of Canaries tourism is a package arrangement consisting of a furnished apartment or villa. The cost is often little more than the normal airfare. But arrangements usually have to be made well in advance.

Other forms of accommodation

Hotel-residencia and **Hostal:** With a few luxurious exceptions, these are modest hotels, often family concerns. They are also graded by stars (one to three). A three-star *hostal* usually costs about the same as a two-star hotel.

Pensión: Boarding house, graded 1 to 3, with few amenities.

Fonda: Village inn, clean and unpretentious.

Parador: Government-run hotel, normally in isolated regions, operating at a loss to encourage tourism. Usually excellent accommodation at bargain prices, often in an unrivalled scenic situation or in a historic building.

a single/double room with bath/shower	**una habitación sencilla/doble con baño/ducha**
What's the rate per night?	**¿Cuál es el precio por noche?**

LANGUAGE. The native language of Canary Islanders is Castilian, the official language of Spain. The accent is slightly different from that on the mainland. For instance, islanders don't lisp when they pronounce the letters *c* or *z*. The language of the Canaries is spoken with a slight lilt, reminiscent of the Caribbean. Indeed, a number of New World words and expressions are used. The most commonly heard are *guagua* (pronounced "wa-wa"), meaning bus, and *papa,* meaning potato.

In tourist areas German, English and, to a lesser extent, French are understood. Because of a great influx of Scandinavian tourists, basic Swedish is now much more likely to be useful in the Canaries than in most European resorts. And in some restaurants and bars Finnish is in daily use.

L | Good morning/Good day | **Buenos días**
| Good afternoon/Good evening | **Buenas tardes**
| Good night | **Buenas noches**
| Goodbye | **Adiós**

The Berlitz phrase book, SPANISH FOR TRAVELLERS, covers most situations you're likely to encounter in your travels in Spain and the Canaries. In addition, the Berlitz Spanish-English/English-Spanish pocket dictionary also contains a menu-reader supplement.

LAUNDRY and DRY-CLEANING. Most hotels will handle laundry and dry-cleaning, but they'll usually charge more than a laundry or a dry-cleaners. You'll find do-it-yourself launderettes in a few areas.

Where's the nearest	**¿Dónde está la lavandería/**
laundry/dry-cleaners?	**tintorería más cercana?**
When will it be ready?	**¿Cuándo estará lista?**

LOST PROPERTY. The first thing to do when you discover you've lost something is obviously to retrace your steps. If nothing comes to light, report the loss to the Municipal Police or the Guardia Civil.

| I've lost my wallet/handbag/ | **He perdido mi cartera/bolso/** |
| passport. | **pasaporte.** |

M | **MAPS and STREET NAMES.** Since General Franco died, Spain has been undergoing a formidable upheaval in many domains. One manifestation is in street names, many of which are being changed, causing a tourist considerable confusion.

Places now sometimes have two names, an old one in honour of a hero of the Franco period, and a new one that pays tribute to a hero of history.

Maps cannot unfortunately keep up with this development, so, with the above in mind, it's worth enquiring immediately of a local inhabitant if you can't find a certain street you're looking for.

A useful map of all seven main islands, plus city maps of three principal cities, is issued by Firestone Hispania.

Car hire firms often provide their customers with simplified maps of the main roads but these are inadequate for anyone wishing to explore the byways of the islands.

| a street plan of... | **un plano de la cuidad de...** |
| a road map of this island | **un mapa de carreteras de esta isla** |

MEDICAL CARE. By far the best solution, to be completely at ease, is to take out a special health insurance policy to cover the risk of illness and accident while on holiday. Your travel agent can also fix you up with Spanish tourist insurance (ASTES), but it is a slow-moving process. ASTES covers doctors' fees and clinical care.

These islands of eternal springtime are supposed to be conducive to longevity, but not if you eat and drink too much or overdo the sun-bathing. Many tourists from northern climes suffer painful sunburns because of first-day eagerness to tan. Take the sun in short doses for two or three days. Another all-too-common problem is the agony of a hangover. Some visitors find the inexpensive liquor too cheap to believe. As for drinking water, play safe and stick to bottled mineral water to avoid "tourist tummy" (see WATER).

A list of local doctors with some knowledge of foreign languages is available at local tourist offices. There are hospitals in all the principal cities and first-aid stations in lesser towns.

Pharmacies *(farmacia)* are usually open during normal shopping hours. After hours, at least one per town remains open all night, the *farmacia de guardia.* Its location is posted in the window of all other *farmacias.*

Where's the nearest (all-night) pharmacy?	**¿Dónde está la farmacia (de guardia) más cercana?**
I need a doctor/dentist.	**Necesito un médico/dentista.**
I've a pain here.	**Me duele aquí.**
sunburn	**quemadura del sol**
sunstroke	**una insolación**
a fever	**fiebre**
an upset stomach	**molestias de estómago**
insect bite	**una picadura de insecto**

MEETING PEOPLE. The Spanish, as a whole, are one of the world's most open and hospitable people, easy to talk to and approach, generous to a fault. *"Mi casa es tu casa"* is commonly heard—and meant.

On the other hand, you might on occasions find the noise level of conversations somewhat deafening. But what you perhaps take for a quarrel is more often than not simply news and gossip being transmitted… passionately.

Spain was long the bastion of a strict moral code; chaperons were no joke, nor was a person's honour. Times—and customs—are changing fast, but fundamental attitudes persist in some forms, even now.

M This is why prudence is recommended for foreign men in their approaches to Spanish women. It also partially explains why Spanish men consider foreign women as fair game. They are often accosted with *piropos*, extravagant compliments. One, addressed to a foreign young woman by a Latin wooer, ran "For you, I would cross the Mediterranean on a shrimp's whiskers!" The word *piropo* comes from the Greek and means "fire in the face", which is how a girl is supposed to look when she's been treated to a romantic approach by a perfect stranger. The tone and gestures may be passionate but it's all harmless.

MONEY MATTERS

Currency: The monetary unit of Spain is the *peseta* (abbreviated *pta.*), which technically is divided into 100 *céntimos*.

    Coins: 1, 5, 10, 50 and 100 pesetas.
    Banknotes: 100, 500, 1,000 and 5,000 pesetas.

    A 5-peseta coin is traditionally called a *duro*, so if someone should quote a price as 10 duros, he means 50 pesetas. For currency restrictions, see ENTRY FORMALITIES AND CUSTOMS.

Banks open from 9 a.m. to 2 p.m. Monday to Friday, and from 9 a.m. to 1 p.m. on Saturdays, but watch out for those obscure holidays which always seem to crop up in Spain! Outside normal banking hours, many travel agencies and other businesses displaying a *cambio* sign will change foreign currency into pesetas. The exchange rate is a bit less favourable than in the banks. Both banks and exchange offices pay slightly more for traveller's cheques than for cash. Always take your passport with you when you go to change money.

Credit cards: All the internationally recognized cards are accepted by hotels, restaurants and businesses in Spain.

Eurocheques: You'll have no problem settling bills or paying for purchases with Eurocheques.

Traveller's cheques: In tourist areas, shops and all banks, hotels and travel agencies accept them, though you're likely to get a better exchange rate at a national or regional bank. Remember always to take your passport with you if you expect to cash a traveller's cheque.

Paying cash: Although many shops and bars will accept payment in sterling or dollars, you're better off paying in pesetas. Shops will invariably give you less than the bank rate for foreign currency.

Prices: Because the Canaries have low luxury taxes, there are astonishing bargains in many luxury items. But as the islands are comparatively far from Europe, many necessities of life cost more there than in mainland Spain.

The good news is that cigarettes, liquor, cameras, tape recorders, typewriters, calculators and perfumes—whatever their country of origin—are big bargains by anybody's standards.

Where's the nearest bank/currency exchange office?	**¿Dónde está el banco más cercano/la oficina de cambio más cercana?**
I want to change some pounds/dollars.	**Quiero cambiar libras/dólares.**
Do you accept traveller's cheques?	**¿Acepta usted cheques de viaje?**
Can I pay with this credit card?	**¿Puedo pagar con esta tarjeta de crédito?**
How much is that?	**¿Cuánto es?**

NEWSPAPERS and MAGAZINES *(periódico; revista)*. Major British and Continental newspapers are on sale in the Canaries the day after their publication. U.S. magazines are available, as well as the Paris-based *International Herald Tribune.* The Canary Islands' English monthly *Island Gazette* keeps you abreast of local interests and attractions, as do the Spanish daily papers published in the islands.

Have you any English-language newspapers?	**¿Tiene periódicos en inglés?**

PHOTOGRAPHY. Beware of lighting situations you may never before have encountered—especially the blinding reflections from the sea or sand dunes or white houses. Read your instruction book carefully or, before leaving home, discuss the problem of shutter speeds and filter accessories with your camera dealer.

All popular film makes and sizes are sold in the Canaries at bargain duty-free prices. 24-hour processing is widely available for both black-and-white and colour film, except Kodachrome which must be forwarded to Madrid for processing.

If you want to buy a new camera, the Canaries are the place to do it. The low prices are tempting. But you may have to hunt around a bit if you insist on a particular make or model.

P I'd like a film for this camera.

Quisiera un carrete para esta máquina.

a black-and-white film	**un carrete en blanco y negro**
a colour-slide film	**un carrete de diapositivas**
a film for colour pictures	**un carrete para película en color**
35-mm film	**un carrete treinta y cinco**
super-8	**super ocho**

How long will it take to develop (and print) this film?

¿Cuánto tardará en revelar (y sacar copias de) este carrete?

May I take a picture?

¿Puedo sacar una foto?

POLICE (*policía*). There are three police forces in Spain. The most famous, and most recognizable, are the *Guardia Civil* (Civil Guard) who wear those distinctive patent-leather hats. Each town also has its *Policía Municipal* (municipal police) who wear different kinds of uniforms depending on the town and season, but mostly blue or grey. Exceptions are the traffic police of Santa Cruz de Tenerife and Las Palmas, Gran Canaria, with their bright, natty costumes and white pith helmets. The third force, the *Policía Nacional,* a national anti-crime unit, can be recognized by their brown uniforms and black berets. All policemen are armed. If you need police assistance, feel free to call on any of these forces. Spanish police are efficient, strict and particularly courteous to foreign visitors.

Where is the nearest police station?

¿Dónde está la comisaría más cercana?

PUBLIC HOLIDAYS (*fiesta*)

January 1	*Año Nuevo*	New Year's Day
January 6	*Epifanía*	Epiphany
March 19	*San José*	St. Joseph's Day
May 1	*Día del Trabajo*	Labour Day
July 25	*Santiago Apóstol*	St. James' Day
August 15	*Asunción*	Assumption
October 12	*Día de la Hispanidad*	Discovery of America Day (Columbus Day)
November 1	*Todos los Santos*	All Saints' Day
December 8	*Inmaculada Concepción*	Immaculate Conception
December 25	*Navidad*	Christmas Day

Movable dates:	*Viernes Santo*	Good Friday
	Lunes de Pascua	Easter Monday
	Corpus Christi	Corpus Christi

P

In addition to these Spanish national holidays, many purely local and lesser religious, civic or apparently irrelevant holidays are celebrated in various towns of the archipelago (see FESTIVALS, page 80).

RADIO and TV *(radio; televisión).* Most hotels have television lounges where the Canaries TV channels may be seen. Most programmes are relayed from the mainland without noticeable loss of quality. All are in Spanish.

R

Travellers with short-wave radios will be able to pick up the BBC World Service and the Voice of America very clearly at night and in the early morning hours. A radio station in Las Palmas broadcasts brief news and music programmes in English, German and Swedish, mornings and evenings. Another station on Tenerife broadcasts twice daily in the same languages.

RELIGIOUS SERVICES *(servicio religioso).* The national religion of Spain is Roman Catholic. Masses are said in almost all the churches of the Canary Islands, including those of outstanding artistic or historical interest.

In the principal tourist centres, Catholic services are also held in foreign languages.

Catholic and Protestant services in various languages are organized regularly in the new Ecumenical Temple of Maspalomas, Gran Canaria.

There is an Anglican church in Taoro Park, Puerto de la Cruz, Tenerife, and in Ciudad Jardín (Garden City), Las Palmas, Gran Canaria.

There are no synagogues in the Canary Islands.

SIESTA. The word has become universal. Unfortunately, the custom hasn't. But in the Canaries, try a rest after lunch. It may be one of Spain's greatest discoveries.

S

You'll find most shops and offices closed between 1 and 4 p.m. (They make up for it by remaining open till 7 or 8 p.m.)

TIME DIFFERENCES. In winter the Canaries maintain Greenwich Mean Time, which is one hour behind the time in most European countries (including mainland Spain). For the rest of the year the

T

T islands go on summer time (daylight saving time), as does Spain—keeping the one-hour difference.

Winter time chart					
Los Angeles	Chicago	New York	London	**Canaries**	Madrid
4 a.m.	6 a.m.	7 a.m.	noon	**noon**	1 p.m.

What time is it, please? **¿Qué hora es, por favor?**

TIPPING. Since a service charge is normally included in hotel and restaurant bills, tipping is not obligatory. However, it's appropriate to tip bellboys, filling-station attendants, bullfight ushers, etc., for their service.

The chart below gives some suggestions as to what to leave.

Porter, per bag	35 ptas.
Maid, per week	150 ptas.
Waiter	10–15% (optional)
Taxi driver	10%
Hairdresser/Barber	10%
Tourist guide	10%

TOILETS. There are many expressions for toilets in Spanish: *aseos, servicios, W.C., water* and *retretes.* The first two terms are the most common.

Public conveniences are rare except in the big cities of the Canaries, but all hotels, bars and restaurants have toilets. It is considered polite to buy a cup of coffee or a glass of wine if you drop in specifically to use these conveniences.

Where are the toilets? **¿Dónde están los servicios?**

TOURIST INFORMATION OFFICES *(oficina de turismo).* Information about the Canary Islands may be obtained from Spanish National Tourist Offices, maintained in many countries.

Canada: 60 Bloor St. West, Suite 201, Toronto, Ont. M4W 3B8; tel.: (416) 961-3131.

United Kingdom: 57–58, St. James' St. London SW1 AILD; tel. (01) 499-0901.

U.S.A.: 845 N. Michigan Ave., Water Tower Place, Chicago, IL 60611; tel. (312) 944-0215.

665 5th Ave., New York, NY 10022; tel.: (212) 759-8822.

Casa del Hidalgo, Hypolita & St. George Streets, St. Augustine, FL 32084; tel.: (904) 829-6460.

1, Hallidie Plaza, Suite 801, San Francisco, CA 94102; tel.: (415) 346-8100.

Fortaleza 367, P.O. Box 463, San Juan, PR 00902; tel.: 725-0625.

These offices will supply you with a wide range of colourful and informative brochures and maps in English on the various towns and regions in the Canaries. They will also let you consult a copy of the master directory of hotels in the islands, listing all facilities and prices.

On the spot there are official tourist information offices in the islands.

Principal locations:

Santa Cruz de Tenerife: Plaza de España; tel. 24 22 27
Puerto de la Cruz, Tenerife: Plaza de la Iglesia; tel. 37 19 28
Las Palmas de Gran Canaria: Parque Santa Catalina; tel. 26 46 23

Where is the tourist office?   **¿Dónde está la oficina de turismo?**

TRANSPORT

Boat services: Inter-island boat schedules tend to be flexible. They are published in local papers. Between Tenerife and Gran Canaria there are usually several sailings a day. A jetfoil service also operates between the two islands. Service to the lesser islands often requires changing boats and long delays.

Bus services: Except on the less populous islands, Canaries bus services range from adequate to excellent. Certain long-distance lines offer reserved seats in comfortable coaches. Whether on local or express buses, be sure to retain your ticket throughout the journey. An inspector, wearing his rank with great severity, will probably board the bus at some point to re-check all the paper-work.

Prices and procedures vary from island to island; it's best to inquire at the local bus station about timetables and tickets.

Canaries bus queues are well disciplined but line up in the reverse order from British queues, that is, facing the direction in which they hope to travel. You always board the bus by the front door. Just inside there will often be a turnstile, which merely counts the passengers;

T you buy your ticket from the driver or the conductor sitting behind a little booth, according to the type of bus.

Taxis*: The letters *SP* on the front and rear bumpers of a car don't stand for Spain; they mean *servicio público*. The car is a taxi. It probably has a green light in the front window and a taxi sign as well. In some tourist centres it's likely to be a meticulously polished limousine with a meter inside. Fares are reasonable by European and American standards.

For longer trips there are non-metered tourist cars. Normally there are standard rates for tourist excursions, but check in advance.

Hail a passing taxi, go to a taxi rank or have your hotel receptionist call a cab. Day or night, it's no problem in the Canaries.

Where is the (nearest) bus stop?	**¿Dónde está la parada de autobuses (más cercana)?**
When's the next bus/boat for…?	**¿A qué hora sale el próximo autobús/barco para…?**
I want a ticket to…	**Quiero un billete para…**
single (one-way)	**ida**
return (round-trip)	**ida y vuelta**
Will you tell me when to get off?	**¿Podría indicarme cuándo tengo que bajar?**
Where can I get a taxi?	**¿Dónde puedo coger un taxi?**
What's the fare to…?	**¿Cuánto es la tarifa a…?**

W **WATER** *(agua)*. When Spaniards drink water, it's almost invariably bottled water, not tap water. The most popular mineral water in the Canaries is *Firgas* from a local spring. If you're particularly sensitive to changes of water, watch out for the ice cubes in drinks.

a bottle of mineral water	**una botella de agua mineral**
fizzy (carbonated)	**con gas**
still	**sin gas**
Is this drinking water?	**¿El agua es potable?**

Y **YOUTH HOSTELS.** While there aren't any youth hostels in the Canaries, pennywise holidaymakers of any age will easily find other lodging available at really low rates. See HOTELS, or CAMPING for those who prefer to rough it.

SOME USEFUL EXPRESSIONS

yes/no	**sí/no**
please/thank you	**por favor/gracias**
excuse me/you're welcome	**perdone/de nada**
where/when/how	**dónde/cuándo/cómo**
how long/how far	**cuánto tiempo/a qué distancia**
yesterday/today/tomorrow	**ayer/hoy/mañana**
day/week/month/year	**día/semana/mes/año**
left/right	**izquierda/derecha**
up/down	**arriba/abajo**
good/bad	**bueno/malo**
big/small	**grande/pequeño**
cheap/expensive	**barato/caro**
hot/cold	**caliente/frío**
old/new	**viejo/nuevo**
open/closed	**abierto/cerrado**
here/there	**aquí/allí**
free (vacant)/occupied	**libre/ocupado**
early/late	**temprano/tarde**
easy/difficult	**fácil/difícil**
Does anyone here speak English?	**¿Hay alguien aquí que hable inglés?**
What does this mean?	**¿Qué quiere decir esto?**
I don't understand.	**No comprendo.**
Please write it down.	**Por favor, escríbalo.**
Is there an admission charge?	**¿Se debe pagar la entrada?**
Waiter!/Waitress!	**¡Camarero!/¡Camarera!**
I'd like...	**Quisiera...**
How much is that?	**¿Cuánto es?**
Have you something less expensive?	**¿Tiene algo más barato?**
Just a minute.	**Un momento.**
Help me, please.	**Ayúdeme, por favor.**
Get a doctor, quickly.	**¡Llamen a un médico, rápidamente!**

Index

An asterisk (*) next to a page number indicates a map reference. For index to Practical Information, see also page 103.